INVOKING

the Ancient Gods

in You

Invoking
the Ancient Gods in You:

Star Myths for
all our
Multiple Personalities

David Warner Mathisen

BEOWULF BOOKS   PASO ROBLES, CALIFORNIA

Published by Beowulf Books, Paso Robles, California 2023

This book is not intended as a substitute for the medical recommendations of physicians, mental health professionals, or other healthcare providers. Rather, it is intended to offer information to help the reader cooperate with physicians, mental health professionals, and healthcare providers in a mutual quest for optimum well-being. We advise readers to carefully review and understand the ideas presented and to seek the advice of a qualified professional before attempting to use them. The author and publishers disclaim as far as the law allows any liability arising directly or indirectly from the use or misuse of the information contained in this book.

Mathisen, David Warner.

Invoking the Ancient Gods in You: Star Myths for all our Multiple Personalities /

David Warner Mathisen.

1. Mythology. 2. Astronomy. 3. Spirituality.

ISBN 979-8-9891464-0-6

Thank You

to those Framers of the Myths given to All Nations

to all of my teachers throughout my life

and to all of my family

This Book is Dedicated

to the

Healing of Trauma

and to the

Restoration of Liberty

the Elimination of Oligarchy

and the Return of Odysseus through

the Guidance, Inspiration and Love of the Goddess

Contents

Introduction

Out of all the classes we had to take when I was a cadet at the US Military Academy at West Point, psychology was among my least favorite.

At that time I was only 18 or 19 years of age, and not particularly "self aware," to put it kindly. My dislike of psychology could perhaps be partly attributed to a rather uninspiring course curriculum, but that would hardly explain the visceral dislike that all things psychology inspired in me at that age. It can perhaps be better understood by the line from Shakespeare's *Hamlet* which says, "The lady doth protest too much, methinks" (Act 3, scene 2), meaning in this case that psychology hit a little "too close to home" for me at that age.

In retrospect, I now believe that psychology is one of the most important and intriguing subjects we can explore in our lives, and one of the most applicable. My lifelong love of ancient myth led me eventually to the discovery (not that I am the first to discover it, by any means) that the world's myths are based on the stars and heavenly cycles, connecting sacred traditions across cultures and all the way around the globe — but once the evidence to support this conclusion piles up to the point where it is conclusive and irresistible, we are still left with the question: "But why?"

What is the purpose or reason behind basing the sacred stories on the stars? The question was particularly pointed for me personally, because at the time of my life when I began to perceive the overwhelming evidence that the world's myths — including the stories contained in the Bible, from the book of Genesis all the way to the book of the Revelation — are based on celestial metaphor, I myself had been taking the Bible literally as a devout literalist Christian (and one, I might add, who was gravitating steadily towards more and more intense and severe theological positions). If the Bible stories were in fact based on the stars and heavenly cycles, with figures such as Moses and Jesus and David and Solomon all corresponding to specific constellations in the sky, and the stories of their various adventures and actions understandable based on the other constellations and heavenly features around them, then what was their point and their purpose? The discovery that the figures and events described in the stories certainly undermines the conventional literal interpretation which teaches that they are relating the lives of historical, terrestrial figures — but what then would be the purpose of such elaborate celestial metaphors?

The more I explored the connections between the stars and the myths, the more I became convinced that they are employing these intricate and beautiful and dramatic and often even haunting stories as a vehicle for conveying to our understanding profound truths about ourselves, about our own internal landscape and experience. And as I examined the myths across cultures stretching from ancient Mesopotamia to the K'iche' Maya of modern-day Guatemala, I began to realize that the recurring pattern of twins and twinning — such as we find, for example, in the Gilgamesh epic between the hero Gilgamesh and his near-twin Enkidu, or in the stories of the Popol Vuh about the hero-twins Hunahpu and Xbalanque — are not talking about two different individuals, but rather are dramatizing something about us, about our own selves, and about a kind of "split" or division between an ordinary or "lower" or ego self (typified by Enkidu, who like Jacob's twin brother Esau in the Genesis story is described as being distinctly "hairy") and a higher Self. The myths, I began to realize, were trying to awaken us to the existence of this higher Self, and to point us towards the reality of such a Self in our own lives.

I had already written several books totaling thousands of pages, some of them exploring this concept of higher Self explicitly (such as 2017's *Astrotheology for Life* and 2019's *Ancient World-Wide System*) when I first encountered the pioneering work of Dr. Gabor Maté, whose work over the course of many years with men and women suffering from addictions convinced him that addiction and addictive behaviors in every single case have to do with a desperate attempt to mitigate and self-medicate the pain and heartbreak of deep trauma, often childhood trauma — and his assertion that psychological trauma describes the process by which we become alienated from our own authentic Self.

I immediately perceived that what cutting-edge healers such as Dr. Maté, and others to whom he would sometimes refer in his talks, such as Dr. Peter Levine and Dr. Bessel van der Kolk, were discovering and articulating corresponded to what the ancient myths were dramatizing over and over again!

I also began to realize that what they were describing had powerful application to my own personal journey throughout my life — including almost certainly my decision to attend the Military Academy in the first place, which is a rather extreme environment to seek out at the age of 17, which is how old I was when I flung myself into it on the first of July in 1987, a few days before my 18th birthday. What was I looking for when I walked into that institution, with its tradition of severe hazing of first-year cadets and its requirement for years of subsequent active-duty service in the regular army following graduation? What was I looking for when I gravitated towards the parachute team at West Point and spent virtually every waking hour (outside of the required classes and athletic and military activities) skydiving out of the big bay-doors of Vietnam-era Huey helicopters, and occasionally angering my parachute team coaches with "low-pull" episodes, in which I would freefall lower than the specified safety altitude before pulling my chute? What compelled me to select the 82nd Airborne Division as my first duty station after West Point, and choose to become an officer in the Infantry, with its requirement for every officer to attend Ranger School after graduation?

In retrospect, and with the benefit of the perspective gained so many years later by listening to the wisdom of healers including Dr. Gabor Maté, I realize that I was looking insistently and intently and certainly intensely for something — and that the "something" that I was looking for was actually my Self.

Shortly after graduation from West Point in 1991, the movie *Point Break* starring Patrick Swayze, Keanu Reeves and Lori Petty was released (on 10 July of 1991, in fact, a week after my 22nd birthday and just over a month after the graduation of the Class of '91 on the first of June). Already being addicted to skydiving and to a lesser extent to surfing, I felt that the film had been practically written expressly to appeal to me, and it became an immediate favorite. I saw it in the theaters and later owned it on videocassette (well before the arrival of movies in digital form) and watched it many dozens of times over the years.

There are some very revealing lines in that film which, with the benefit of the perspective provided by the work of Dr. Maté, become extremely significant to the question of Self, separation from Self, and searching for recovery of Self. In one important scene, the character of Tyler (played by Lori Petty) says to Johnny (played by Keanu Reeves) with obvious concern that she hopes he's not "buying into" the extreme vision offered by Bodhi (played by Patrick Swayze) and his followers, involving ever-more-extreme activities and one-upmanship. Johnny, who apparently has not thought about it, asks Tyler what she means. She replies: "You've got the kamikaze look, Johnny. I've seen it. Bodhi can smell it a mile away."[1]

Here, "the kamikaze look" is obviously shorthand for increasingly dangerous and even potentially self-destructive or self-sacrificing behavior, and Tyler says it in the scene just after the camera pans across a close-up view of photographs on the wall showing Bodhi and others engaged in freefall skydiving, rock-climbing and surfing. Just after she says it, Bodhi himself enters the room and declares, "Johnny's got his own demons, don't you, Johnny?"[2]

Both Bodhi and Tyler recognize that Johnny is searching for something — and Bodhi has already hinted that he knows exactly what Johnny is searching for, at the conclusion of an earlier scene in the movie, in which Bodhi tells Johnny: "You still haven't figured out what riding waves is all about, have you? It's a state of mind. It's that place where you lose yourself and you find your Self — and you don't know it yet but you got it, and it's right there." As he says "it's right there," Bodhi points right to Johnny's forehead.[3]

Johnny didn't know it, but he was looking for something — he was looking to find his own Self — and he was increasingly attracted to the intense lifestyle Bodhi was offering because he sensed that it might somehow lead to "that place where you lose yourself and you find your Self."

Looking back at my own 22-year-old self, it seems pretty clear that I was pursuing similarly intense activities in search of something — and that at the time I too was not consciously aware of what I was looking for, or why I was doing it.

A few years later, I threw myself intensely into literalist Christianity — no doubt, I am now convinced, in continuation of the same search. At the time, I did not of course know that the scriptures of the Bible, in common with the other ancient myths and sacred stories of cultures around the world, are actually *metaphorical* in nature, using an esoteric approach to dramatize for us truths which we might otherwise be unable to grasp, or which we might, in fact, resist and reject, because we have psycho-logical "defense mechanisms" which keep us from facing them. It can be demonstrated with quite conclusive evidence that the myths of the world, including the stories of the Bible, have as one of their core central themes the trauma of separation from Self, and the path to recovery of Self. Even if we are not consciously aware that this theme is at the heart of these stories, we can be drawn to them because we sense it without overtly perceiving it.

But if someone tells us that separation from Self is at the core of the stories, we might vehemently reject it, because separation from Self is a very painful subject, if we ourselves have actually become alienation from Self. As Dr. Maté and others explain, separation from Self is the result of intense pain, shame, guilt, or heartbreak, often occurring in early childhood and often suppressed and buried because the heartbreak is so painful and so difficult that we do not want to be reminded of it, and don't want to even admit that it has happened.

Unfortunately, even if we are drawn to the stories of the Bible because we perceive instinctively or unconsciously that they hold the secret to understanding separation from Self and even point the way towards recovery of Self, the literalistic interpretation of those stories can not only obscure their core message but can actually *invert* it. Instead of being about healing from trauma and recovering the very Self to whom we already have access, right inside of you, literalistic interpretations actually tend to inflict more trauma, and point to "externalized" solutions, which are ultimately no solution at all.

After perceiving that the stories of the Bible are metaphorical and deeply connected to all the other ancient myths and sacred stories of cultures around the world, I have personally found that in understanding their inherently esoteric nature we lose none of the "good" aspects of the Biblical texts (in other words, what probably attracted us to them in the first place), but we only "lose" the negative aspects which are traumatizing and divisive, dividing up the family of mankind (by insisting that the Bible stories, and only the Bible stories, are exclusively "true," while the sacred stories and traditions of all other cultures are not only wrong but actually evil) and dividing ourselves internally as well (through the doctrines of the Fall and Original Sin and Total Depravity and the threat of eternal punishment in the fires of a literal Hell).

When I encountered the work of Dr. Gabor Maté in May of 2019, just a few weeks after publishing *The Ancient World-Wide System*, and realized that the things that pioneering modern healers such as Dr. Maté and trauma-focused psychologists such as Dr. Peter Levine were teaching about trauma, separation from Self and suppression of Self parallels what the myths are dramatizing in their stories, I began a new book to explore the new insights that this understanding could give to the ancient myths of the world, which became *Myth and Trauma*, published in 2020.

Since that book's publication, I have only become more and more convinced that the ancient myths have as one of their absolutely central themes our alienation from our own Self and the path to recovery, and of their vital relevance for our lives today, in this very present moment. I am convinced that one of the reasons that the myths use metaphor and an esoteric approach (in which we are shown the lesson before we even grasp its full meaning, in much the same way that Mr. Miyagi teaches Daniel-san karate in the first *Karate Kid* movie) is that we have strong psychological defense mechanisms which deny and resist facing the whole idea of separation from Self, in order to avoid probing wounds which are still too painful to touch.

And, as my understanding has continued to evolve since writing *Myth and Trauma*, I realize that there is even more to the story. Through some of the talks and podcasts with Dr. Maté that I have listened to over the years, I encountered the work of psychologist Dr. Richard Schwartz, whose Internal Family Systems paradigm explains that our inner landscape is even more complex than the more familiar "binary" divide of "lower self" (or "egoic self") versus "higher Self" that we might first expect when looking at the world's countless myths depicting twins and twinning (from Castor and Pollux, to Heracles and Iphicles, to Jacob and Esau, and even to Jesus and Doubting Thomas, as I explore in *Myth and Trauma*).

Dr. Schwartz's work, as we will explore in this volume, suggest that we are all actually more accurately understood as "multiple" rather than as "binary" — and that understanding opens a whole new perspective on what the ancient myths of the world are trying to tell us, and to dramatize for our benefit through their amazing, fantastic, unforgettable, and sometimes bizarre and frankly shocking stories.

This work, which you now hold in your hands, continues the investigation and updates the evolution of my understanding of the myths that have taken place since the publication of *Myth and Trauma*. I very much hope that it will be of some benefit to you, and that it will encourage you to further explore the incredible treasure of ancient wisdom given to each one of us in the world's ancient Star Myths, which are in fact all about you.

Victoria, Australia

09 September, 2023

Chapter One

The gods in you

"From the Heliconian Muses let us begin to sing, who hold the great and holy mount of Helicon, and dance on soft feet about the deep-blue spring and the altar of the almighty son of Cronos [. . .] Thence, they arise and go abroad by night, veiled in thick mist, and utter their songs with lovely voice [. . .]. Hail, children of Zeus! Grant lovely song and celebrate the holy race of the deathless gods who are forever, those that were born of Earth and starry Heaven and gloomy Night and them that briny Sea did rear."   — Theogony[4]

The sacred texts of ancient Greece begin with an invocation of the divine — a calling to the Muse or the Muses by the poet, with the expectation that the Muse will come when invoked, and speak through the one who has called upon her. The opening lines of the ancient text of the Theogony are cited above, but the opening lines of the Iliad and the Odyssey and of the Works and Days all open with a similar invocation to the Muse or to the nine Muses.

What does it mean? How is it that we can call upon the goddess and she will appear?

Other ancient myths preserved in different cultures around the world also indicate that gods can appear in a moment when invoked. In the Norse myths, for example, we see evidence that the god Thor will appear instantaneously when his name is called by those in need (see for example the story of the rebuilding of the walls of Asgard, recounted in the Prose Edda in the section known as the Gylfaginning).

In the sacred writings of ancient India, we find the story of the child Dhruva, which is recorded in the Bhagavata Purana. In that ancient text, we learn of a king named Uttânapâda, who as king was strictly charged with "the protection and maintenance of the world." In a pattern found throughout the world's myths, the king has two wives in this story. According to the Bhagavata Purana, the king's two wives are named Sunîti and Suruci, and when we encounter the family in the story, each of the wives has a young son by the king. The son of Sunîti is named Dhruva, and the son of Suruci is named Uttama.

However, the king favors one wife over the other -- he dotes upon Suruci and neglects Sunîti. Suruci for her part jealously promotes her son at the expense of Dhruva in the affection of the king. Thus, one day when Dhruva, the son of Sunîti, attempts to climb up on his father's lap to join Uttama the son of Suruci, Suruci sees Dhruva and rebukes him, telling Dhruva he does not deserve to sit on the lap of his father the king, saying:

> "My dear child, you do not deserve to seat yourself where the
> king sits because, even though you were born as a son of the

king, you were not born from my womb. Oh child, you do not understand that, because you are not my own but were born from the womb of another woman, the thing you desire is out of your reach. You can seat yourself on the throne of the king if you want, but only if you, by means of penance, have satisfied the Original Person of God and thus by his mercy have secured a place for yourself in my womb."[5]

The text tells us that Dhruva, whom we later learn to have been five years old at this time, is devastated by these harsh words, and even more so by the fact that his father the king is looking on and says nothing in the face of this rejection. The child is filled with anger and begins to breathe "as heavily as a snake struck by a stick," according to the text, and he runs to his mother, weeping with emotion at the rejection.

Sunîti of course is very sad to see her son Dhruva in such a state, and she comforts him and lifts him to her lap. Not knowing what else to say, the text tells us that she advises the boy to seek out the very Lord of Transcendence himself, the one who is beyond the reach of blunt instruments, and advises Dhruva to fix his mind upon the divine image of the god, thinking of nothing else.

Getting himself under control, we are told, Dhruva leaves his mother and the palace and heads out to follow her advice. On the way, he encounters the great sage or Rishi named Nārada, who is a great musician and carries in one hand a khartal (a percussive instrument resembling a castanet) and in the other a tanpura (a long-necked stringed instrument resembling a lute). Nārada is sometimes known as Rishiraj, or the king of all sages.

Nārada asks Dhruva where he is going, and he is so impressed by young Dhruva's answer, as well as Dhruva's respectful tone and earnest desire to meditate upon the Supreme Lord and to follow the path advised by Dhruva's mother that the sage gives the boy his blessing and directs the child to go to the bank of the river Yamuna in the sacred Madhuvana forest, and to practice *pranayama* (control of the breath or Prana) and meditate upon the merciful Supreme Lord Vasudeva while reciting a mantra. The mantra which Nārada imparts to Dhruva, which the sage tells the boy is a "most confidential mantra," *Om namo bhagavate vasudevaya.*

Having been thus advised, we are told, young Dhruva circumambulates respectfully around the great sage, and performs the proper obeisance to his reverence, and proceeds deep into the forest to the banks of the river Yamuna, where he begins to meditate upon the divine person of the Lord Vishnu (the name Vasudeva usually applies to one of the aspects of the god Vishnu, as well as being sometimes applied to the god Krishna, who himself is one of the avatars of Vishnu).

There, after meditation and recitation of the mantra, and also standing upon one leg, the text tells us that Dhruva was blessed with a visit from the Lord Vishnu himself, who imparts to Dhruva blessings and promises for the child's future, including the promise that Dhruva will one day become a great king himself, ruling wisely for the benefit of all the people, a king who at the end of his life will even ascend to the stars of heaven.

As with so many of the world's ancient myths, the reader might be forgiven for thinking, "This story is about some extremely blessed and gifted child, who lived thousands of years ago in a place and time far removed from my own -- what can it possibly have to do with me? It is all very good that Dhruva was so enlightened that he could seek out and gain a vision of the

Infinite, but that is because he was very special, a child unlike anyone who has ever lived before or since!"

But as we can demonstrate beyond any reasonable doubt with the ancient myths and sacred stories of cultures around the world, the story of Dhruva and his encounter with the god can be seen to be esoteric and metaphorical in nature, based upon the stars of the night sky.

Those who have read my 2019 book *The Ancient World-Wide System* will know that the god Vishnu can can be definitively identified with the constellation Ophiuchus, an extremely important and pivotal constellation about whom we shall have much more to explore going forward. The famous ancient Sanskrit texts describing Vishnu reclining upon the great multi-headed serpent Shesha (also known as the Sheshanaga and the Nagaraja, the King of All Serpents), dreaming the universe into existence while floating upon the primordial ocean, with a lotus-plant growing out of Vishnu's navel, can be confidently shown to correspond to the constellation Ophiuchus above the form of the constellation Scorpio, which itself appears to be "floating" or swimming in the widest and brightest part of the Milky Way galaxy, and which often plays the role of a multi-headed serpent in numerous myths around the world:

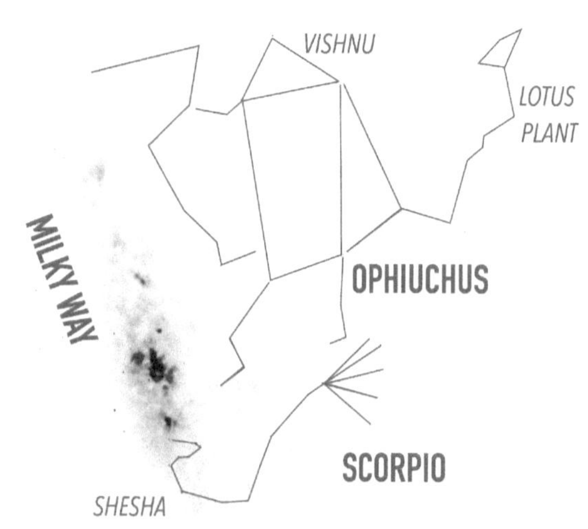

The fact that Vishnu appears to young Dhruva beside the river Yamuna no doubt refers to the fact that Ophiuchus (which we can see to be associated with Vishnu) is actually situated in the sky directly adjacent to the Milky Way — in fact, adjacent to that same brightest part of the Milky Way in which Scorpio is also swimming, the wide part of our galaxy known to modern astronomers as the Galactic Center. The band of the galaxy, in this case, corresponds to the river Yamuna in the myth, beside which Dhruva stands when he invokes Vishnu.

Below is an example of one of many images depicting Dhruva reciting the mantra given to him, until the god appears before him:

So, if Vishnu is associated with Ophiuchus and the river Yamuna is associated with the Milky Way band itself, what constellation plays the role of the five-year-old Dhruva, calling to the god using the mantra given to him by the Rishi?

Interestingly, although we might initially guess that the constellation Sagittarius would play the young son of the king, being a constellation which is located beside the Milky Way on the opposite "shore" from Ophiuchus, and much smaller in size than the constellation Ophiuchus itself (just as Dhruva is probably much smaller than the god Vishnu), the details of the Bhagavata Purana indicate that Dhruva stands on one leg while reciting his mantra, and that Dhruva also will one day ascend to the heavens after his life is over and become a pivot around which all of the other stars of heaven will turn.

As I have argued in *The Ancient World-Wide System*, this evidence points to the conclusion that Dhruva too is associated with Ophiuchus! Myths in which a figure associated with Ophiuchus is described as standing on one leg are not uncommon in the world's ancient myths, both from ancient India and from other cultures, and Ophiuchus itself is a constellation which acts as a kind of "pivot" in the esoteric language of the world's ancient sacred traditions.[6]

What does this surprising connection tell us? For one thing, it provides yet another example of an ancient myth which indicates that the gods will appear in an instant when they are properly invoked, just as we saw in the earlier examples from the Norse myths and the Greek myths. But even further, it hints at the truth that the gods can appear in an instant because they are already present with us — that they are in fact in some way available to us at all times, because the gods are already in us! If Dhruva is calling to Vishnu, and if Vishnu is associated with Ophiuchus but Dhruva himself is also Ophiuchus, then it seems that in some way Vishnu appears to Dhruva when properly invoked because *Vishnu is already there*, present with Dhruva already.

But is there any support for such an astonishing conclusion? Do we find other evidence among the world's ancient myths and sacred traditions for the idea that the gods are actually present with us at all times — that they are indeed "in us" somehow, working out their will through us in some synergistic way?

Indeed we do.

In fact, abundant evidence points us towards that exact conclusion. In the myths of ancient Greece, for example, in addition to the invocations which begin so many important ancient mythological texts (which, as we have already seen, imply that the Muse is ready to speak through the poet, when she is called upon), we also see numerous ancient accounts describing the priestess of Delphi, through whom the god Apollo speaks his prophecies to those who approach the sacred temple in search of guidance. We shall have more to say about the important Oracle at Delphi and its priestess, who was known as the Pythia according to the ancient accounts, but for now it is enough to simply note that the god of Delphi was always described as speaking *through* her, supporting the conclusion that the gods work their will through men and women, and indeed that they in some sense *dwell in* men and women.

Elsewhere in the Greek myths, we can see numerous examples of gods and goddesses inspiring men and women, and yet (as I discuss at some length in my 2020 book *Myth and Trauma*) in one of the most interesting and revealing instances of such divine inspiration, described in the Odyssey when the hero Odysseus has been cast into the sea, his raft having been destroyed by a powerful storm unleashed by the god Poseidon, and on the morning of the third day Odysseus is trying to find a place to make landfall along the rocky shores of the land of the Phaeacians, powerful waves crashing against sharp cliffs threaten to dash him to pieces, the text describes the hero's thoughts as they veer towards panic, until we read that the goddess Athena "prompted his mind" and gave him prudence to calm down and assess the situation — as if she is in his actual thoughts, directing them.[7]

The goddess does not actually reach down and rescue Odysseus in the dangerous situation: instead, she is described as calming his thoughts and thus imparting some divine inspiration to him — and then Odysseus himself must take it from there, swimming parallel to the shoreline until he finds a safer place to try and turn towards land. When reading this event in Book Five of Odyssey, the only way we know that this inspiration is from Athena (as opposed to being from the hero's "own thoughts") is that the text itself attributes the "prompting" in the mind of Odysseus as coming from the goddess.

This pattern of a god or goddess appearing at the moment of need and imparting inspiration or guidance to the hero, who must then actually go forth and do the appropriate action himself, occurs elsewhere in the Odyssey — and throughout the myths of ancient Greece. In the myth of Medusa (which was also featured in the discussion in *Myth and Trauma*, and about which we will also have more to explore later in this volume), when Perseus confidently sets off on his quest to find the lonely island of the Gorgons, Athena and Hermes appear and give the young hero guidance and gifts. And while the ancient accounts are clear that Perseus could never have succeeded in this task without the inspiration and gifts imparted by these gods, it still remained to Perseus to actually accomplish the entire arduous mission with skill and courage and bring it to its successful end.

From this pattern we can deduce that the gods provide their aid *from within us* in some way, when we are ready to listen to them, or when we deliberately invoke them by calling upon them in the appropriate manner.

And we can go still further with this line of investigation and see evidence from ancient sacred tradition which suggests that not only do the gods work their will through us but that we can also embody the divine and take on their power, just as the poet takes on the inspiration of the Muse who speaks through the one who invokes her.

Far across the globe from Greece, we find the ritual opera of China, thought to have originated at least as early as the Tang period (not later than 712 CE), and which continues to this day in various forms, including Cantonese opera.[8] In this tradition, the performers are understood to be performing their art *for the gods*, within a ritual sacred space which is set apart from ordinary reality, and as they assume their various roles, the actors become imbued with (or even possessed by) the spirit of the deity or the legendary figure whom they are portraying on the sacred stage. As scholar and researcher of Asian art and culture Dr. April Liu has explained in her 2019 book *Divine Threads: The Visual and Material Culture of Cantonese Opera*,

> Cantonese opera troupes observe many ritual practices and taboos associated with costuming. These practices reflect the widely shared view that operas occupy a liminal space between earthly and spirit realms. Once in full costume, the performers are in direct contact with the spirits and thus imbued with numinous powers. As they step through the stage curtains, they pass from the ordinary realm and into a

realm of spirits where they embody the "ghosts" of historical figures and the presence of immortal deities. As anthropologist Barbara Ward observes, the performers are "not merely players" but also ritual specialists and shamans who directly channel the presence of spirits for the benefit of the human community.[9]

The above section of Dr. Liu's book begins with a quotation from the accomplished Su Dongpo (1037 – 1101, also known as Su Shi), a renowned poet, painter, author, calligrapher and public figure who lived during the Song dynasty, who observed: "To perform as the ancients is to pass in and out of the realm of ghosts (*banyan guren shi, churu guimendao*)."[10]

In this ancient operatic tradition, the performances are actually enacted for the gods, who are understood to be in attendance. The actors paint their faces in specific patterns as they take on the identity of the god or ancient personage, and according to strict tradition each actor must apply the makeup himself or herself. The similarity of this tradition to the donning of special masks identified with specific supernatural beings by the shamans of various cultures around the world has been noted by more than one commentator.

Traveling yet again nearly all the way across the Earth, this time across the vast Pacific to the continent of North America, we find the same concept of *the gods being present in us* expressed in the *Katsinam* (or Kachina) tradition of the Hopi and Zuni Nations of Indigenous cultures inhabiting the lands of the Colorado Plateau, in the region of present-day New Mexico and Arizona.

In her 1991 book *Kachina Dolls: the Art of Hopi Carvers*, author and former Arizona State Museum photographer Helga Teiwes writes:

> The Hopi have refused to have their religion taken away from them. They believe in living their own way, the Hopi Way. They call themselves Hopiitu, the friendly or peaceful people. The Hopi overcome difficulty or adversity not by aggression and open conflict but by considering all the elements in nature and adapting to new situations in a nonviolent manner. Living this way takes spiritual strength, which the Hopi seek in complex religious ceremonies and prayers to their deities, whom they approach through intermediaries. These intermediaries are the *Katsinam*, the Spirit Beings of the Hopi world [a footnote in the original text here explains: "In this book, the term *Katsina* refers to the spirit itself (plural *Katsinam*), and *kachina* refers to the doll carved to depict the spirit"]. Hopi scholar Emory Sekaquaptewa says that "the katsinam are the heart of Hopi life." They are the beings to whom all Hopi look for direction, heed, and give their prayers for the continuation of life — not only their own life but also life in general, for Hopi benedictions include all life on this planet.[11]

The important point of focus for our discussion in this chapter is the fact that those who take on the role of *Katsinam* in the Hopi and Zuni and related Puebloan Native American nations themselves *become* — while they are wearing their sacred mask and paint and ornaments — *Katsinam* themselves. The supernatural beings enter into the dancers, and thus those who are impersonating the *Katsinam* themselves *become* those beings, while they are wearing their ritual costumes. This concept is very reminiscent of what we just observed in the tradition of Chinese opera.

In her 1939 book *Pueblo Indian Religion*, anthropologist and folklorist Dr. Elsie Clews Parsons wrote:

> When the dancers put on masks, they not only impersonate the kachina but they *are* kachina, just as when Keresan doctors draw on their bear paws, Bear comes into them and they become bears, with the healing power of Bear. When the clowns paint at Zuni with mud from their sacred spring, they identify themselves with their patron or prototype, Paiyetamu, the Youth, the first of the Ne'wekwe or Koshare, son of Sun Father or of underground Mother, who is funny and so senseless that his father has to let him do just as he pleases. Through their priests, their doctors, and their sacred clowns and dancers Pueblos are in close contact or accord with their Spirits.[12]

In reading various accounts discussing those who take on the role of a Katsina, one finds one English word frequently used for those who do so is "impersonator." While in common usage this word may have negative connotations of deception and connivance, if we simply look at the word itself, it seems highly appropriate. The word *im-personating* could be taken as indicating the "person-ing" of the Spirit through the individual who is "in-person-ing" that Spirit. The person receives the identity of the deity or spirit power, thus "personing" the spiritual being.

Such examples can be multiplied as we continue around the world. Indeed, it is likely we could find examples preserved in the received traditions of virtually every culture. The Yoruba people of Western Africa were taken in enormous numbers as slaves to the Americas and in particular to the Caribbean, where they preserved their knowledge of their ancestral gods and spirit beings, known as Orisha. I have elsewhere demonstrated that, for instance, the Yoruba thunder and fire god Xango (also spelled Shango and Chango) has numerous characteristics in common with other sky-and-thunder-related gods around the world, from Zeus of Greece to Thor of the Norse to Chahk of the Maya.

Intriguingly, one way that the supernatural Orisha of the Yoruba express themselves is through dance, with different Orisha being recognizable by the dances which they express through men and women at different times. In the traditions of Santería, which developed in the Caribbean region among the Yoruba diaspora in the centuries following and continues the observation of the original West African gods of the Yoruba culture, practitioners can enter states of ecstatic trance during which they are inhabited by Orisha. During these ecstatic states, the ecstatic practitioner often exhibits specific dance movements which enable those present to identify the particular Orisha who is directing the movements of the one thus possessed.

Here is a description by author and Santería scholar Mary Ann Clark from a chapter on Santería in the 1998 study *Sects, Cults and Religious Traditions: A Sociological Analysis* describing this process:

> In Santería, the medium is taken over by a spirit who can bless, lecture to, and dance with the congregation. Individ-

uals can approach the embodied *Orisha* with their problems, and the *Orisha* can single out individuals or families for particular messages, blessings, or warnings. During the time of the possession event, devotees believe that the gods are truly incarnated and walk with them. [. . .] The most common venue for possession is the religious party called a *tambor* or *bembé*. These celebrations are community fiestas in honor of a specific *Orisha*. [. . .] Each *Orisha* has its own particular set of rhythms, songs, and dance movements. As a particular *Orisha*'s rhythm is played, the song leader and congregation sing. *Santeros* who are priests and priestesses of that *Orisha* dance in the open space in front of the drums. The songs are designed to call the *Orisha* down to take possession of one of those dancing. When a dancer begins to show signs of possession (more intense dance movements, jerky or irregular movements, "spacey" or contorted facial expressions), the energy of the group focuses upon him or her until the *Orisha* is firmly "seated." Once the possession process is complete, the dancer no longer exhibits his or her personal mannerisms, reflecting instead the mannerisms of the *Orisha*.[13]

While some might object that we cannot use modern-day Santería as evidence of an ancient understanding that the gods can dwell within and exercise their will through men and women, it is widely acknowledged that the Orisha themselves who are still recognized in Santería are Yoruba deities who are also known in the western parts of Africa. And, while it may be argued that in the hundreds of years since the days of the slave trade and the diaspora of the Yoruba people, remarkable confirmation that the ancient understanding has been preserved without interference over the centuries of diaspora and enslavement exists in the fact that the dance movements associated with specific deities can be seen to correspond to the celestial figures with whom I argue that those deities are also associated.

For example, as noted above, I have argued that the thunder-god Shango can be seen to be associated with the constellation Hercules in the night sky — as can other thunder-gods or rain-gods from other cultures around the globe. Shango's distinguishing characteristics include his powerful axe and his fearsome property of issuing fire from his mouth when he speaks. Additionally, as described by folklorist William R. Bascom (1912 – 1981) in his 1980 book *Sixteen Cowries: Yoruba Divination from Africa to the New World*, "his thunderbolts are prehistoric stone celts which farmers sometimes find while hoeing their fields; they are taken to Shango's priests, who keep them at his shrine in a plate supported by an inverted mortar, which also serves as a stool when the heads of initiates are shaved."[14]

From these and other details about Shango and his various adventures, we can confidently identify this god with the constellation Hercules. One of the distinguishing features of mythical figures associated with Hercules is a powerful weapon, including a thunderbolt weapon such as that associated with Thor, Zeus, Indra, and other sky-gods. Shango is also described as hurling thunderbolts. This powerful weapon can be seen in the outline of the constellation Hercules in the sky, as shown below:

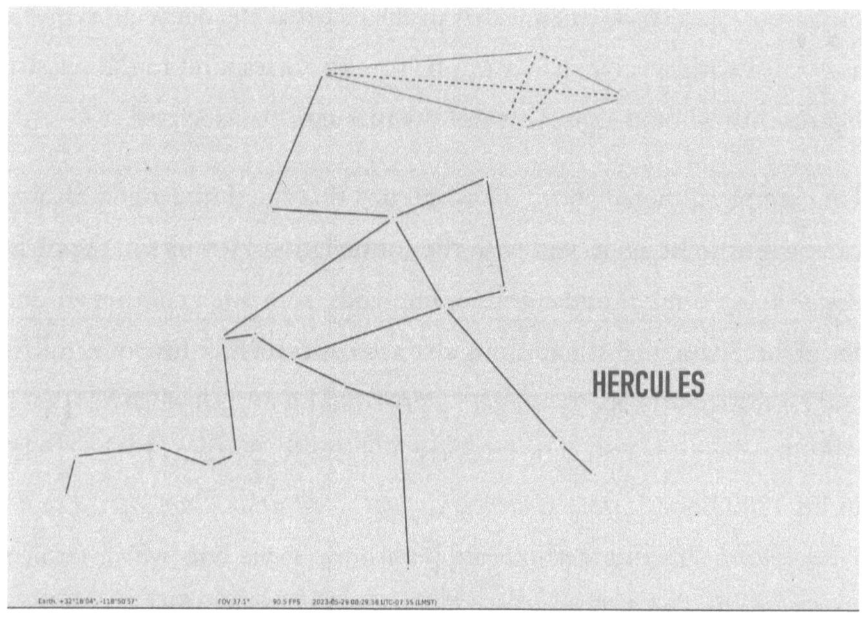

As with other star charts shown in this volume, the above diagram comes from the free and open-source digital planetarium app, *Stellarium*. Colors are inverted in order to show more clearly on the printed page: everything dark in the sky is light in the image (in other words, the background night sky appears light instead of dark), and everything light in the sky shows up as dark in the image (particularly the stars, which appear as small black circles instead of as white points of light, with larger dots on the page indicating brighter stars in the sky). The connecting lines, of course, are not actually visible in the sky but are "sketched-in" using our imagination — and the outlines generally follow those suggested by H. A. Rey (1898 – 1977) in his indispensable book *The Stars: A New Way to See Them* (first published in 1952), as discussed in previous books including at some length in *Myth and Trauma*.

In the above close-up study of the stars of the constellation Hercules, I have taken care to show the location of each star by deliberately *not* drawing the connecting lines in a continuous fashion, but stopping short of each star so you can see its location. Note the distinctive features of the outline: deep lunging posture, with rear leg very extended and rear heel raised, front knee also deeply bent, square-shaped head (sometimes suggesting a man with a full beard, as with the god Zeus or his son Heracles or Hercules, and also as Shango is sometimes depicted in woodcarving), one arm held menacingly overhead and brandishing a weapon, and the other arm reaching forward (this other arm seemingly emanates from the "bottom corner" of the square-shaped head).

Below are two images of sky-gods who can be positively identified with this constellation in the night sky, from different cultures separated from each other by several thousand miles of distance as well as by the mighty gulf of the Atlantic Ocean, as well as by many centuries of time. The first, on the left, is the god Zeus, from artwork found on an ancient vase dating to roughly 540 BCE. We can clearly see the same deep lunging posture with heel raised, as well as one arm held menacingly overhead (brandishing a thunderbolt) and the other reaching forward. On the right, we see artwork depicting the rain-god Chahk (also spelled Chaak by some scholars) of the Maya, painted on a cylindrical tumbler thought to date from around the eighth century CE:

Remarkably, we can see the very same posture in the artwork depicting the god Chahk that we see used in the artwork depicting the god Zeus. The deep lunge position of the legs and body of Chahk match the stars of the constellation almost perfectly:

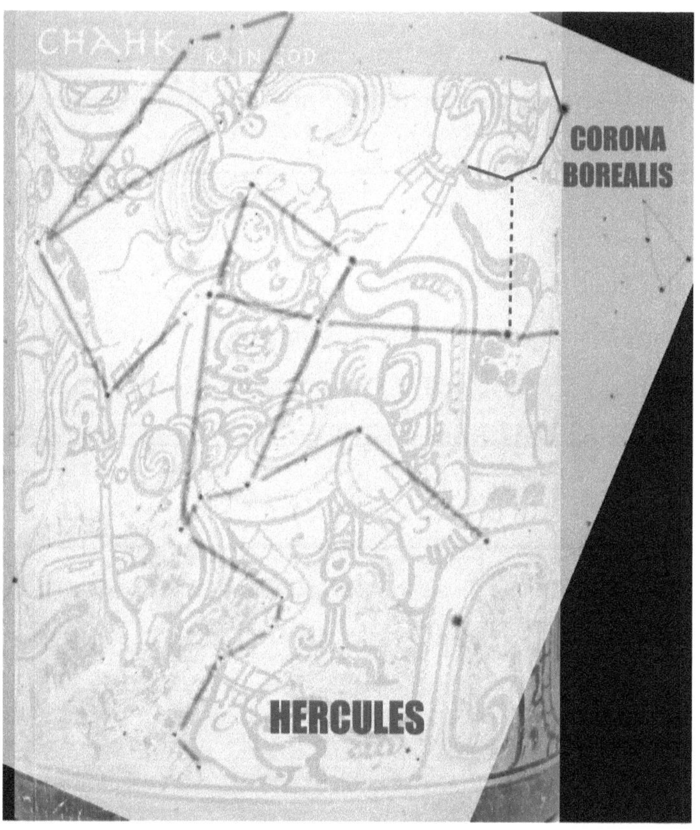

As I have demonstrated elsewhere previously, the artwork on the Maya cup also includes the forward arm of Chahk grasping a disc. Scholars disagree about the identity of the disc-shaped object that Chahk is grasping, but I have no doubt about its identity: it is an object representing the constellation Corona Borealis (which means the Northern Crown), located directly in front of the constellation Hercules in the night sky, and often grasped by mythical figures associated with the constellation Hercules.

Note that Chahk is depicted carrying an axe, which he is brandishing over his back, held by the hand on the other side of his body from the hand that is grasping the disc. This is very significant, because the axe is also the chosen weapon of the god Shango of the Yoruba, who is, like them, a sky- and storm-god.

In the close-up of the stars of the constellation Hercules shown below, I show how the weapon being brandished can be seen to be an axe instead of a club or a sword. In the diagram, I have indicated the position of four stars in the "sword" which could be envisioned as forming the head of an axe:

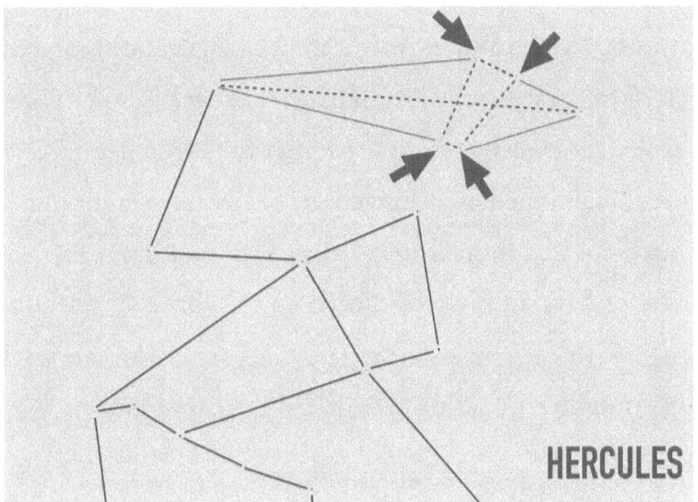

I have connected these four small stars with a dotted line to indicate the outline of the axe, and drawn a longer "axis" through the head of the axe, running from the star that represents the end of the upraised arm to the star that could also be envisioned as indicating the "tip of the sword," if the weapon were to be envisioned as a sword instead of an axe. From these dotted lines, you should be able to see how the weapon brandished over the head of Hercules could be envisioned as an axe, as carried by the gods

Chahk and Shango. Note well that this same outline could also suggest a hammer, and we can think of another powerful thunder-god who carries a mighty hammer instead of an axe: the god Thor of Norse mythology, who is also associated with the same constellation Hercules, as I have argued in my 2018 book *Star Myths of the World, Volume Four: Norse Mythology*.

The above details should establish that Shango, in common with other powerful sky-related deities around the world, is associated with the constellation Hercules. Abundant other evidence supports this conclusion, including the detail given by William Bascom in the previously-cited quotation explaining that when thunder-stones are found in the fields, they are taken to a Shango shrine where they are kept "in a plate supported by an inverted mortar, which also serves as a stool when the heads of initiates are shaved." As I discuss at some length in *The Ancient World-Wide System*, there is abundant evidence from myth that the constellation Ophiuchus is sometimes envisioned as an "inverted" or overturned mortar. Because Ophiuchus is located immediately below Hercules in the sky, it is quite appropriate to have an inverted mortar in the shrine of an Orisha who is associated with the constellation Hercules, where he can reach down towards the thunder-stones that are placed there for him.

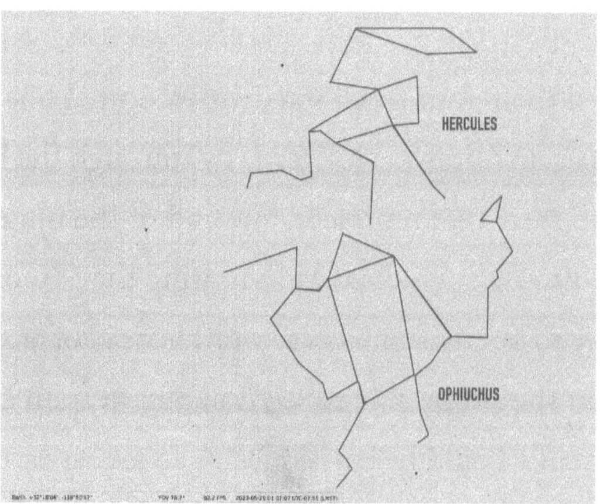

Most intriguingly, once we understand that Shango is associated with the constellation Hercules, we can see the incorporation of *characteristics of this constellation* in the traditional dance forms which are associated to this day with Shango in the Yoruba-influenced culture of Santería!

There are many videos on YouTube, as well as a number of documentaries and National Geographic-style studies discussing the connections between the Orishas and dance, which show the characteristic movements of Shango. Below are just two screenshots from different videos selected from YouTube showing the dance associated with Shango or Chango:

As can be immediately seen, the dance moves associated with Shango feature deep lunges very evocative of the outline of the constellation Hercules itself, as well as powerful upraised arm gestures. Sometimes the dancer even carries an axe, as seen in the top image.

The expression of the Orishas of the Yoruba through men and women in dance constitutes yet another example establishing beyond doubt that myths and sacred traditions around the world show us that the gods dwell in men and women, and work out their will through men and women. They are with us and indeed in us, ready to be invoked when called upon by one who will "im-person-ate" them.

Note that in the top image the dancer has a grimacing facial expression during this powerful, lunging move in the Shango dance — indeed, he appears to be sticking out his tongue to enhance the impact of his fierce grimace. Recall that fire comes out of the mouth of this Orisha when he speaks: William Bascom writes of Shango that "He was noted for his magical powers and was feared because when he spoke, fire came out of his mouth."[15]

It can be shown that around the world, figures associated with the constellation Hercules (as we can now confidently say for the thunder-god Shango) are often depicted or described as having a grimacing face, staring eyes, and sometimes a protruding tongue as well. Below, for example, is a statue of the Japanese god (or Kami) named Zao Gongen, a powerful god who, like Zeus and Jupiter of ancient Greece and Rome, and like Indra of the Vedas of ancient India, is often described and depicted as carrying a thunderbolt-weapon (a Vajra, which in Japanese is called a Kongosho):

Note once again the distinctive lunging body posture which indicates an association with the constellation Hercules (an indication which is confirmed by a variety of additional evidence, including the aforementioned Vajra or Kongosho, as well as his association with mountaintops, upon which he is almost invariably depicted in Japanese artwork — a connection which I would explain as further evidence that he is associated with the constellation Hercules, which stands in the sky directly above the constellation Ophiuchus, which often takes the role of a mountain in myths around the world, just as we earlier saw that it can be envisioned as an "inverted mortar").

Zao Gongen is always depicted with a grimacing mouth and wide-staring eyes, which is a facial expression common to figures associated with the constellation Hercules in cultures around the world. Below is an image of a Gorgon, from artwork on an Attic vase of ancient Greece dated to around 520 to 510 BCE:

Once again we see the distinctive lunging posture characteristic of the constellation Hercules, and I have elsewhere argued that there are a number of additional details which confirm the association, including the fact that in many instances of ancient artwork depicting Gorgons, the fringe of serpentine hair around a Gorgon's head resembles a man's beard or even a lion's mane — and note that other mythical figures associated with the constellation Hercules (such as Thor of the Norse and Zeus and Heracles himself from the Greek myths) will commonly have a full beard, due (I argue, as briefly mentioned above) to the fact that the constellation itself has a distinctly square-shaped head. The hero Heracles (or Hercules, as he was known to the Latins) also commonly wears a lion-skin head over his own head, and thus when we see Gorgons depicted with their hair forming a lion-like "mane," we can see that this fact further confirms their association with the constellation Hercules:

In the plate above, thought to date to around 600 BCE, the "leonine" beard is clearly visible on the Gorgon head. These details should be sufficient to establish the fact that the ancient Gorgons of myth are associated with the constellation Hercules, at least in some instances (although I have argued that there are reasons to conclude that their mortal sister, Medusa, who unlike the Gorgons was turned into a monster after being born as a mortal woman, is undoubtedly associated with the constellation Andromeda).

Note that in both of the ancient Gorgon images above, the staring eyes and grimacing mouth are clearly visible, and in both cases the tongue is protruding. This facial expression of staring eyes and grimacing mouth with protruding tongue is indeed characteristic of Gorgons when depicted in ancient artwork. We will see why this facial expression is so significant in a moment, but first have a look at this photograph taken during the Second World War of men from the Maori Battalion of New Zealand performing a *haka* in the sands of North Africa:

A haka is a Maori traditional dance often involving vigorous movements accompanied by rhythmic percussive shouts and deep lunges — as well as facial grimaces involving wide-staring eyes and extruded tongue. As can be seen from the image above, haka often begin with the participants kneeling on one knee, and making arm gestures symbolic of powerful striking moves or even (as in the image above) reminiscent of a thunderbolt weapon! The connection of this ritual dance to the constellation Hercules is unmistakable, as is its similarity to some of the movements associated with the dance of the Orisha Shango of the Yoruba.

English naturalist and botanist Joseph Banks, who was part of the expedition of the *Endeavour* under Lieutenant (later Captain) James Cook from 1768 through 1771, describes the haka that he witnessed in New Zealand in his journal, providing details about the facial grimaces, widened eyes, and protruding tongue:

> The war-song and dance consists of various contortions of the limbs, during which the tongue was thrust out incredibly far, and the orbits of their eyes enlarged so much that a circle of white was distinctly seen round the iris; in short, nothing is omitted which could render a human shape frightful and deformed, which I suppose they think terrible. During this time they brandish their spears, hack the air with their patoo-patoos [hand-held weapons, generally in the shape of clubs], and shake their darts as if they meant every moment to begin the attack, singing all the while in a wild but not disagreeable manner, ending every strain with a loud and deep-drawn sigh, in which they all join in concert. The whole is accompanied by strokes struck on the sides of the boats with their feet, paddles, and arms; the whole in such excellent time, that though the crews of several canoes join in concert, you rarely or never heard a single stroke wrongly placed.

This we called the war-song; for though they seemed fond of using it upon all occasions, whether in war or peace, they, I think, never omitted it in their attacks.[16]

Note the clear similarities between the description of the staring eyes and protruding tongue, and the artwork we have seen of mythical figures associated with the constellation Hercules. The god Tiki of Aotearoa (New Zealand) and other islands of the Pacific can also be seen to demonstrate the same characteristics associated with the constellation Hercules, including the staring eyes and protruding tongue. In the carving below, from Aotearoa, the god Tiki is depicted with these distinctive features, and note that the god is brandishing a club-shaped weapon overhead (a clear characteristic of figures associated with the constellation Hercules), and appears to be depicted in something of a lunging posture, also characteristic of the same constellation — indeed, very similar to the divine force being embodied in the ritual dance of the haka shown above in the photograph from World War II:

Thus, we can hardly avoid the conclusion that through the performing of the haka, those participating are embodying, indeed "person-ing" or "in-person-ating," the deity himself, and expressing his power and strength and other attributes, just as the *Katsinam* dancers of the Hopi and Zuni take on the attributes of the supernatural beings of their cultures, and just as the performers in the Chinese operas take on the attributes of the gods, spirits, and ghostly ancestors whom they are in-person-ing in their ritual dramas.

As Joseph Banks notes in his early description of the haka, the Maori perform haka for occasions other than for the preparation of combat — but he also notes that in his observation, they never prepare for battle *without* doing a haka first. The performance of the haka — and thus the in-personing of the attributes of the powerful being with the staring eyes and protruding tongue, with his deep lunges and brandished weapon, associated like so many other powerful gods such as Zeus and Thor and Shango with the constellation Hercules in other cultures around the globe.

Are there any attributes of this constellation which can explain the extending of the tongue that we see in the haka, and which is also associated with the Gorgons of ancient Greece (whose posture and other symbology can be seen to associate them, too, with the same constellation)?

Indeed, there are!

When we look at the outline of the constellation Hercules, which by now we have seen several times, we can observe that while one arm is held menacingly overhead and brandishing a powerful weapon (which sometimes appears in myth as a club, or as a sword, or as a thunderbolt-weapon of some description), the other arm is extended forward, and appears to originate at the bottom of the square-shaped head of the constellation:

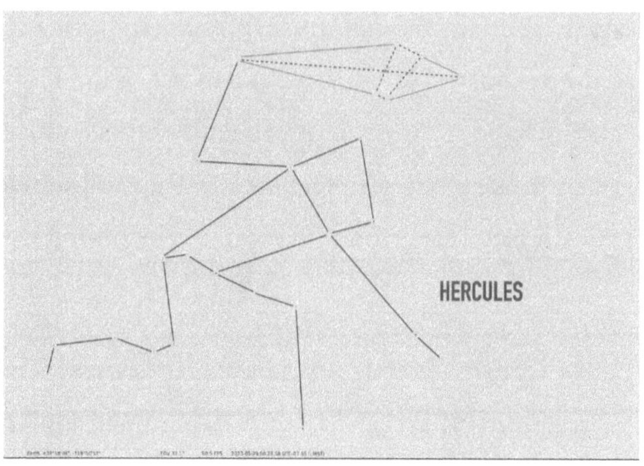

It is my contention that this "forward-reaching arm," which protrudes from the base of the square-shaped head, can be envisioned as an extended tongue! Note that we have seen evidence of this protruding tongue in the ancient artwork depicting Gorgons from Greek myth, and we have also seen that Shango of the Yoruba was feared in part because fire would emanate from his mouth when he spoke. We also saw abundant evidence that grimacing facial expressions are often associated with figures connected to Hercules, including Zao Gongen of Japan, as well as Shango himself (including dancers when they are "in-personing" the god), and now the figures of Tiki and those performing the haka.

Intriguingly, in the Yoga traditions of India, whose practices have been shown to stretch back to ancient times, there is a posture or *asana* (literally, "seat" or "sitting posture") known as *simhasana*, or "lion pose." This asana is described by B. K. S. Iyengar (1918 – 2014) in his iconic 1966 book *Light on Yoga* as follows:

(1) Sit on the floor, with the legs stretched straight in front.

(2) Raise the seat, bend the right knee and place the right foot

under the left buttock. Then bend the left knee and place the left foot under the right buttock. The left ankle should be kept under the right one. (3) Sit on the heels with the toes pointing back. (4) Then bring the weight of the body on the thighs and knees. (5) Stretch the trunk forward and keep the back erect. (6) Place the right palm on the right knee and the left palm on the left knee. Stretch the arms straight and keep them stiff. Spread the fingers and press them against the knees. (7) Open the jaws wide and stretch the tongue out towards the chin as far as you can. (8) Gaze at the centre of the eyebrows or at the tip of the nose. Stay in this pose for about 30 seconds, breathing through the mouth. (9) Withdraw the tongue into the mouth, lift the hands from the knees and straighten the legs. Then repeat the pose, first placing the left foot under the right buttock and then the right foot under the left buttock. (10) Stay for an equal length of time.[17]

Note the instructions in point number 7 regarding opening the jaws wide and stretching the tongue towards the chin as far as possible, as well as the instructions in point number 8 regarding the open-eye gaze. Both staring eyes and protruding tongue are characteristic of figures associated with the constellation Hercules, and the fact that practitioners performing the lion pose of Yoga exhibit or "in-person" such characteristics themselves. Below are two images of Yoga practitioners performing versions of simhasana. While neither posture is precisely the same as described by B. K. S. Iyengar in the passage just cited, both photographs show the extended tongue that is associated with Hercules-related figures:

In his discussion of simhasana, B. K. S. Iyengar explains that simhasana is dedicated to Narasimha, "the Man-Lion Incarnation of Vishnu."[18] He explains that the Sanskrit word *nara* means "man" and *simha* means "lion," and then relates a story about a demon-king, Hiranya, who was unable to be killed by man, beast, or deity and who terrorized his kingdom and even his own son, until Vishnu burst forth in the form of Narasimha, neither man nor beast, and tore the demon to pieces. Images of Narasimha slaying the demon-king often feature the lion-headed avatar in a lunging posture with sharply-upraised knee, over which he is bending backwards the body of Hiranya. These details indicate beyond doubt, should any additional evidence be needed, that the "man-lion incarnation" is associated with the constellation Hercules:

Because the ancient artwork shown above is slightly difficult to see, I have

duplicated the original image (which is on the left) and then drawn-in

some rough outlines in the image on the right to show the now-familiar

lunging posture with sharply upraised knee, characteristic of mythical

figures associated with the constellation Hercules. Note that the "arching"

shape of Hiranya is another indication that Narasimha is associated with

Hercules, because Hercules-associated figures in myth are often shown

grasping an arc-shaped object or even a human-shaped figure in a hard

arch. This association comes from the fact that the constellation Corona

Borealis, the Northern Crown, is positioned in the sky just in front of

the forward-reaching arm of the outline of Hercules, and thus figures

associated with the constellation will sometimes be envisioned as grasping

an arc-shaped object or figure, just as we saw with the Maya god Chahk in

the earlier example.

It is quite notable that the hero Heracles himself wears a lion-skin over his

head, with the head of the lion-skin fastened over his own head, just as

the figure of Narasimha has a man-shaped body but a lion-shaped head.

Additionally, in the mythology of ancient Egypt, we find the lion-headed god Bes, shown below in a relief from the region of Dendera:

Note that Bes in the above image is depicted as having a fringe-like lion's beard around his head, in a style very much reminiscent of the artwork of the Gorgons from ancient Greece which we observed earlier. Additionally, of course, Bes is depicted with a protruding tongue!

All of these examples indicate that we are dealing with manifestations of powerful deities connected with the same constellation in the sky, the constellation Hercules, and that ancient myths around the world retain the information that some Hercules gods exhibit grimacing expressions and a vigorously-extended tongue. The fact that we see men and women impersonating these characteristics, such as in the Yoga asana of the lion pose, and in the haka of the Maori of Aotearoa, indicates the presence of an ancient tradition of calling forth or invoking the power associated with these supernatural beings and expressing them in our own lives, including when facing dangerous situations, such as going into battle (which Joseph Banks observed was never done without first performing the haka).

As we conclude this first chapter, then, we can see beyond any doubt that the world's ancient traditions teach that the gods are available to men and women, and in fact that the gods in some sense dwell in us and express themselves through us. We will have much more to say about ways that we can apply this knowledge in our lives for our own benefit and blessing, and that of others, but from what we have seen so far we can already see that the ancient myths demonstrate that we can invoke the gods and that they will appear in response to being called — and indeed the world's ancient traditions indicate that not only *can* we invoke the gods but that we very much *should* do so (recall from the very beginning of this chapter that the ancient epics of Greece, as well as the works of Hesiod and other ancient poems, always begin with an invocation of the Muse).

This invocation can even take the form of dance, as well as Yoga postures such as simhasana with its staring eyes and sharply-extended tongue. Functional dentist Dr. Steven Lin has pointed out that there is a connection between the tongue and the vagus nerve, which is an extremely important cranial nerve which, among other functions, serves to regulate the powerful sympathetic and parasympathetic nervous system responses to stress and dangerous situations (the sympathetic nervous system activates our "fight or flight" responses, while the parasympathetic nervous system acts to return us to a relaxed state after stress or danger, sometimes referred to as the "rest and digest" state).

In a post on social media discussing the connection between the tongue and the vagus nerve, Dr. Lin asks "Was Michael Jordan controlling his vagus nerve by sticking out his tongue?" He writes:

There is an interesting connection between how the tongue calms and primes the brain. The vagus nerve stimulates certain muscles in the heart that help to slow heart rate. [. . .] Signals through the vagus send the chemical to tell the brain to release acetylcholine, an important chemical to slow heart rate. Acetylcholine is basically the heart's natural pacemaker. The connection is significant because when you have good "vagal tone" it is a clinical measure believed to indicate overall levels of vagal activity, but is measured indirectly through the heart rate variability (HRV). [. . .] While the hypoglossal nerve is primarily involved in protruding the tongue, the subsequent activation of the throat muscles and palatoglossal muscle which lifts the back of the tongue to move it out of the throat is innervated by the vagus nerve.[19]

Basketball superstar Michael Jordan was well known for fully protruding his tongue while performing powerful dunks and other basketball shots during competition. Dr. Lin argues that he may have been using this full tongue extension to regulate his vagus nerve in order to calm his nervous system and achieve greater focus.

What is certain is that this same tongue extension can be seen in ancient myth and in the received traditions of Yoga in India and the haka in Aotearoa, and that both traditions appear to be aware of benefits associated with performing this extension. We have also seen that the extended tongue is definitely associated with mythical figures associated with the constellation Hercules, and that figures associated with Hercules are associated with power and with protection — including the figures of

Zeus, Thor, Chahk, Shango, Bes, Narasimha and Tiki. We have also seen that Thor, at least, has a demonstrable tradition of appearing immediately when he is called upon (and the story of Narasimha indicates a similar willingness of the god Vishnu and his various avatars to appear when called upon as well, as does the story of the child Dhruva cited earlier).

Thus, we can conclude that understanding the fact, demonstrated beyond any argument by the ancient traditions of the world that the gods dwell with us and can exert their power through us can be of real benefit in our lives. It may be that extending the tongue while widening the eyes and grimacing is just one way of invoking such benefits. Let's continue this exploration to see more of how learning about "the gods in you" can help us in our daily life, even in this modern age.

Chapter Two

Discord

The verses of Hesiod tell us that the beautiful goddess Thetis was one of the fifty daughters of the sea-god Nereus, who himself was known as the "Old Gentleman" (or the Old Man, hence the Old Man of the Sea) because his temperament is gentle and trustworthy, and because Nereus always acts in accordance with what is right, and always speaks truthfully.[20] Nereus dwells in a grotto at the bottom of the sea and ancient artwork depict him as having a great curving fish-tail, holding a staff, and bearing a cornucopia, from which he pours forth the sea's bounty. The fifty daughters of Nereus and his consort Doris are known as the Nereids, and Thetis seems to be the unofficial leader of the Nereids, according to some ancient accounts.

Thetis became the bride of the mortal hero Peleus, one of the sons of the mythical king of Aegina (or Egina), an island in the Saronic Gulf between the Pelopennese and the Attic Peninsula. Some say she was previously pursued by both Zeus and Poseidon because of her great beauty, but that both of these gods desisted when they learned of the prophecy that Thetis would one day bear a son who would be greater than his father. Because of this prophecy, according to some accounts, the gods arranged for Peleus to win her hand in marriage instead — and that marriage produced the son

Achilles, who would become by far the greatest of the warriors on earth during his lifetime.

Ancient vases depict the gods in procession making their way to the wedding feast of Thetis and Peleus, and an extremely ancient but now lost text known as the Cypria tells the story of that wedding. Even though the Cypria itself is now lost, later writers describe parts of the Cypria's contents, including the description of that wedding of Thetis and Peleus. According to the ancient accounts, all the gods and goddesses of the ancient pantheon attended the feast, but the goddess Eris was purposely excluded from the festivities — for Eris was the goddess of strife and disruption, who was known to the Romans as the goddess Discordia or simply Discord.

Bitter and hurt by this exclusion, Eris made her way to the wedding anyway, without invitation, only to be barred at the door. Vowing to disrupt the joyful banquet from which she had been rejected, Eris took an apple (in some accounts, one of the golden apples of the Hesperides, which grew upon a tree far to the west, even beyond the Ocean) and threw it into the party, with the words "For the Most Beautiful" inscribed upon it. This golden apple with its provocative inscription has come to be known as the infamous "Apple of Discord," which would start a chain reaction leading eventually to the catastrophic Trojan War and the loss of countless lives.

The golden apple of the goddess of strife did its work immediately. The goddesses Hera, Athena and Aphrodite each claimed that the apple should belong to her, leading to such an argument during the banquet that Zeus was asked to settle the question as to which of the three the apple should be awarded. Rather than step into the midst of such a quarrel, Zeus commanded Hermes to bear the apple to the realm of Priam, king of Troy, and find the king's younger son Paris, a graceful youth whose own world-renowned physical beauty would apparently render Paris well-suited to award the apple to the goddess to whom it should belong.

Hermes found Paris tending sheep on the hillsides beyond the walls of Troy, and gave the youth the apple and the command issued by Zeus himself that Paris must judge between the three goddesses and award the prize to the most beautiful. Awe-struck Paris according to some ancient accounts tried to back out of the assignment, but Hermes told the young man that once Zeus had spoken there was no more to be said, and thus Paris had to comply.

And so began the famous "Judgement of Paris," by which Paris decided the case between the three illustrious goddesses: Hera the queen of Olympus and wife of Zeus, Athena the goddess of wisdom and of war for just causes, and Aphrodite the goddess of beauty and desire and sexuality. Most ancient accounts have the judgement itself taking place upon Mount Ida, a sacred mountain of myth, the location of one Mount Ida being outside the walls of the city of Troy (in modern-day Turkey or Turkiye), although there is another Mount Ida on the island of Crete.

The Heroides attributed to Ovid describe the scene from the first-person perspective of Paris himself, who relates that as he reclined against a tree, gazing out over the lofty rooftops of Troy, when the earth seemed to shake and the wing-footed herald of the gods appeared before him, bearing his golden wand. At the very same moment, Paris relates, his eyes were opened to the arrival of the divine trio of goddesses, standing upon the turf of the pastoral hillside, their presence rendering Paris speechless and causing his hair to raise with chill tremors.

"Lay aside thy fear!" Hermes commanded. "Thou art the arbiter of beauty; put an end to the strivings of the goddesses; pronounce which one deserves for her beauty to vanquish the other two!"[21]

Emboldened by the admonition that Zeus himself had chosen Paris to pronounce this judgement, the ancient poem says, the youth was now able to turn his face towards each of the three deities and consider her beauty. "Of winning all were worthy," he relates, "and I who was to judge lamented that not all could win."[22]

At this point, the three goddesses each attempt to sway the young man by offering him a reward in exchange for choosing her. Hera offers Paris the worldly political might — in some versions, the rulership of all of Asia. Athena offers him the gift of valor, and an illustrious lifetime career in battle, if he will award the apple to her. Finally, Aphrodite speaks, and offers the youth the most beautiful woman on earth to be his bride — an offer that Paris finds most attractive of the three. He awards the apple to the goddess of love, and in doing so dooms his own nation to destruction, for the most beautiful woman promised to Paris is none other than Helen, who is already married to Menelaus, king of the Spartans.

Ancient sources including the Iliad describe Helen as the daughter of Zeus, by Leda queen of Sparta. Zeus appeared to Leda in the form of a swan and slept with her, arranging to have her husband Tyndareus, king of Sparta, sleep with her later in order to conceal from Tyndareus that anything was amiss, since Leda would become pregnant due to the encounter. Forty weeks later, the queen bore the legendary twins Castor and Polydeuces (Polydeuces being more familiar to us by his Roman name, Pollux), one of whom (Polydeuces) is immortal and the son of Zeus, and the other (Castor) mortal and the son of Tyndareus. According to some versions of the story, Leda also bears two twin daughters (whether by this union with Zeus and Tyndareus or perhaps by another similar encounter), one of whom (Helen the Beautiful) is the daughter of Zeus, and the other of whom (Clytemnestra) is the daughter of Tyndareus.

Helen's beauty was so famous that when she reached marriageable age, every hero and king wanted to marry her. A competition was arranged, with the agreement that whoever won would marry Helen, and whoever participated but did not win would support the one who did, including the oath that they would fight to win Helen back, if anyone ever stole her from the winning husband to whom Helen would be wed.

Menelaus of Sparta won the competition and took Helen to be his queen. His older brother Agamemnon, king of Argos, married Clytemnestra. When Paris awarded the apple to Aphrodite, however, the goddess arranged for Paris to take Helen the Beautiful to Troy — and when she was stolen away from Menelaus, all the other men who had previously tried for her hand were bound to support Menelaus in his efforts to get her back. Thus was launched the Trojan War, led by Agamemnon and Menelaus, and ending in eventual disaster for Troy.

Recall that the whole thing began with the exclusion of Eris, goddess of strife or Discord, followed by an apple inscribed "To the Fairest of All" or "For the Most Beautiful." Then, the subsequent quarrel between three goddesses who each demanded that she be *publicly acknowledged* as the *most beautiful* led to Zeus commanding that the argument be settled by the decision of young Paris.

The second-century author Apuleius of the North African colony of Numidia (present-day Algeria), himself a neoplatonic philosopher and initiate into the ancient *mysteria*, bewails the decision of Paris to allow his decision to be swayed by the offered bribe of the goddess of beauty, and describes this fateful decision by the young man as "bartering the first judicial decision for the lucre of lust," thereby bringing about the doom of all humanity![23]

This pronouncement, by an ancient author who was privy to the esoteric traditions of antiquity and whose novel *The Metamorphoses* can be seen to be dealing with profound subjects under its rollicking and ribald surface narrative, that the Judgement of Paris was so important that it can be seen in one sense as leading to the fall of all his kind, shows that these ancient myths of "choices" or "judgements" were understood to contain critical lessons for us to understand.

Consider for context two other mythical judgements, that of King Midas and that of King Solomon, when offered gifts by the divine. Midas, offered by the god Dionysus whatever the king requested, foolishly asked that anything he touched would turn to gold, despite the fact that (in the myths) Midas was already fabulously wealthy and had more gold than any other man. What was wrong with this king, that he was still not satisfied, we might ask ourselves. What hole was Midas trying to fill, unsuccessfully, by piling wealth on top of wealth, gold on top of gold?

We might perhaps ask the same of Paris, who was so famously good-looking himself that the gods chose him to arbitrate in the quarrel of the goddesses. Could not a youth of such beauty find a bride who would make him happy, without having to bring about the Trojan War and the fall of his own father's kingdom by abducting Helen, who was already married to another man?

We might even be so bold as to wonder why any of the goddesses, including the very goddess of love and beauty herself, would have been so insecure as to need the confirmation of the Apple of Discord and the public recognition as "the fairest," when of course each of them is already divinely beautiful.

And while the decisions of Paris and of Midas, to ask the divine realm when offered for gold in the one case and the hand of a beautiful woman in the other, are shown by the myths to have disastrous consequences and to incur the disfavor of the gods, the response by Solomon when offered by the divine whatever Solomon might ask (recounted in 1 Kings chapter 3), in the encounter in the great high place at Gibeon, is met with approval. Solomon asks for wisdom and an understanding heart — and wisdom not just for his own benefit, but wisdom to help the people for whom Solomon is responsible, so that he can judge rightly (1 Kings 3: 9). This request, when made by Solomon of the God of the Bible, produces not only approbation from the divine but also a positive outcome — in marked contrast to the disastrous outcomes that result in the myths involving Paris and Midas.

The implication might be drawn from these various myths and their outcomes that our connection to the divine has as its proper object those traits sought by Solomon: specifically "an understanding heart," and the judgement to "discern between good and bad." When we are seeking some sort of self-aggrandizement or self-justification, or (as in the case of the goddesses) desperately-desired recognition from others for something we already possess, we may be headed for strife or even for disaster.

The ancient epic poem of the Iliad tells of the great battle between the Achaeans (the kings and warriors of the people who would later be known as the Greeks), led by Agamemnon and Menelaus, and the warriors and allies of the city of Troy, also known by its ancient name of *Ilion*, or in

Latin *Ilium* (hence the name of the poem). Just as the various cities and islands, from either side of the conflict, send their warriors to the plains of Ilium, so too do the various gods and goddesses line up on either side of the great mythical war, with Aphrodite understandably siding with Paris and thus with Troy, and with Hera and Athena similarly siding against Paris and thus with the forces arrayed behind Agamemnon and Menelaus.

Other gods who aided the Trojans during the conflict include Ares (who was a lover of Aphrodite, even though she was already married to the god Hephaestus), as well as the twins Apollo and Artemis. Helping the Achaeans, in addition to Hera and Athena, were the gods Hephaestus, Poseidon, and Hermes.

While the immortal gods cannot be killed in the conflict, they can suffer injuries, and the verses of the Iliad describe the wounds and subsequent embarrassment suffered by both Aphrodite and Ares by the weapons of the Achaean heroes on the plains of Troy.

The fact that the ancient myths depict the gods in such open conflict with one another is extremely noteworthy, and has tremendous implications for our own lives when coupled with the understanding uncovered in the previous chapter that the gods of ancient myth can be seen to manifest themselves *within us*, and to work out their will *through us*.

Could it be that the gods of the ancient myth not only dwell within us but also, under certain circumstances, line up against one another inside of us, and even fight out their battles on the internal landscapes of our inner terrain?

As this present volume intends to demonstrate, that is *exactly* what I believe the ancient wisdom given to us in the myths is trying to tell us, and that these mythical battles are described for our benefit in order to show us what is going on inside our own individual hearts and minds.

Indeed, the well-known myths involving the origin of the epic war between the Achaeans and the Trojans can be seen to start with the exclusion — we might even say the "exile" — of the goddess Eris, who was left out of the feasting at the celebration of the marriage of Thetis and Peleus, and whose rejection led directly to the quarreling between Hera, Athena and Aphrodite.

This mythological narrative, intriguingly enough, parallels exactly the internal conflicts that modern cutting-edge healers and psychologists have described regarding psychological trauma and attachment injury. Specifically, psychologist Dr. Richard Schwartz, founder of the Internal Family Systems paradigm of understanding trauma and healing (often abbreviated simply as IFS), discovered through the course of working with literally tens of thousands of men and women that all of us have what might be called "multiple personalities," and that having multiple personalities is not at all a "disorder" but is in fact an accurate description of what is going on inside of us at all times. These multiple personalities, or "parts," can become polarized — arranged against one another in their efforts to carry out what they see as their most critical role within the internal family.

Richard Schwartz begins his 2021 book *No Bad Parts* by explaining:

> We were all raised in what I'll call the mono-mind belief system — the idea that you have one mind, out of which different thoughts and emotions and impulses and urges emanate. That's the paradigm I believed in, too, until I kept

encountering clients who taught me otherwise. Because the mono-mind view is so ubiquitous and assumed in our culture, we never really question the truth of it. I want to help you take a look — a second look — at who you really are. I'm going to invite you to try on this different paradigm of multiplicity that IFS espouses and consider the possibility that you and everybody else is a multiple personality. And that is a good thing.[24]

Dr. Schwartz notes that the condition formerly known as Multiple Personality Disorder, now called Dissociative Identity Disorder, arises from extreme abuse resulting in the parts which are a characteristic of every internal system becoming much more polarized towards and disassociated from the other parts within the system. But his experience with thousands of patients in his practice has convinced him that the collection of personalities which each of us carries inside our internal landscape is in fact composed of well-intentioned parts of our own unique mixture of personalities, and that we should see their actions as that of "protectors who are simply trying to keep us safe and are reacting to and containing other parts that carry emotions and memories from past traumas that we have locked away inside."[25]

Citing both his own extensive experience as a psychologist and the work of other doctors and researchers, Dr. Schwartz states confidently that we all have these internal personalities or parts, and that "It's the natural state of the mind to have parts — they are not the product of trauma or of internalizing external voices or energies. It's just the way we're built, and that's good because all of our parts have valuable qualities and resources to give us."[26]

Just like the different gods and goddesses who inhabit the ancient myths and sacred stories given to all the various cultures of the world, these different parts have their own characteristics and their own strengths: valuable qualities and resources to give us, as Richard Schwartz puts it. "They have full range personalities," he says: "each of them have different desires, different ages, different opinions, different talents, and different resources."[27]

Although Dr. Schwartz does not himself directly say that the gods of ancient myth personify our different parts or component personalities, and I do not intend to imply that he says so or that he agrees with me here, look at how his description of our various parts in the sentences cited above lines up with what we could say about the gods of Greek myth whom we have been discussing so far in this chapter (and the gods of other cultures mentioned in this book so far). The gods and goddesses such as Hera and Athena and Aphrodite, Ares and Artemis and Apollo and Poseidon and Hermes and all the rest can be seen, beyond any argument or controversy, to have different desires, different ages, different opinions, different talents, and different resources to give us — just as Dr. Schwartz says in these passages, and just as he and other practicing psychologists who understand and use his Internal Family Systems paradigm have found to be true regarding the multiplicity inside of each one of us.

The gods are most certainly associated with different gifts and different talents. Athena, goddess of wisdom, is the giver of all skill in the arts. The Orphic hymn to Athena calls her "blessed mother of the arts" and says of her "you bring madness to the wicked, you bring prudence to the virtuous."[28] In the famous story of the maiden Arachne, whose skill at weaving was so great that (in the version given to us by Ovid in the Metamorphoses) the very nymphs would leave their mountainside and river haunts in order to watch her graceful movements at the loom.

Ovid writes:

> You would have known / that only Pallas could have been her teacher. / Nevertheless, as though offended by / the very thought, the girl denied it, saying, / "Let her compete with me, and if she wins / I'll pay whatever penalty she sets!"[29]

We see from these lines that the ancient myths themselves dramatize the understanding that certain gifts and talents come from the gods — in this case, skill at weaving being an unmistakable gift from the "blessed mother of the arts" herself. But prideful Arachne refuses to acknowledge the source of her gift. Indeed, Ovid in the telling of Arachne's story relates that it was even said that Arachne "accepted praise that set her above the goddess in the art of weaving,"[30] a woeful affront since Athena herself was the very source and fount of Arachne's skill.

For this grievous inversion of the proper order and her refusal to acknowledge the source of her own fame-bringing gift, Arachne met a fearful end. Challenging Athena herself to a weaving contest, Arachne hangs herself when she loses, and the goddess turns the girl into a spider, to hang and to spin forevermore.

From this well-known episode, we can establish that the gifts we each possess in various mixtures were understood in the myths to come from the various gods. Many other myths describe beautiful maidens whose great beauty of course comes from a divine source but who similarly meet unpleasant fates due to their failure to acknowledge that their beauty is a gift, or who even set their beauty above that of the gods who gave that beauty to them in the first place.

So the assertion that the ancient myths envision our gifts as coming from the gods is well established from evidence, in this instance using well-documented examples from ancient accounts relating stories from Greek mythology, although additional examples from other cultures are quite easy to find as well. In the Sanskrit text of the Mahabharata of ancient India, for example, Arjuna is given gifts by the gods during his visit to heaven, prior to the cataclysmic battle of Kurukshetra, while in the text of the Poetic Edda and other sources of our knowledge of Norse myth we find descriptions of the mysterious goddesses known as the Norns, who apportion aspects of the lives of mortals, and who are described in one poem as arriving at the birth of a hero named Helgi Hundingsbana to bless him with the gifts that will lead him to become the greatest of fighters and wisest of rulers during his life.

What I am working to establish in this chapter is that the different parts of our personality, which in Dr. Richard Schwartz's own words (based upon his experience interacting in the capacity of a professional psychologist with many thousands of men and women) "have valuable qualities and resources to give us," can be understood as our gifts from those gods whose qualities and characteristics are described and portrayed in the ancient wisdom bequeathed to every culture in their myths and sacred stories. If we have exceptional ability in arts and crafts which are associated in Greek myth with the goddess Athena, "blessed mother of the arts," then our unique makeup can be said to have more influence of Athena, while another may have more Aphrodite, and another more Ares, or more Apollo.

Each of us, in fact, contains some mixture of attributes and gifts associated with those deities who personify them — each of us having, in other words, a unique "recipe" of "ingredients" associated with different gods and goddesses. The ancient science of astrology attempts to codify and explain this unique recipe for each individual by looking at the different influences and gifts imparted by positioning of the planets, such as Jupiter and Saturn and Venus, Mars and Mercury, as well as the Sun and the Moon.

As Richard Schwartz explains, our multiple internal parts have their own actual personalities, and to this assertion I would add the observation that the ancient myths clearly portray the various gods and goddesses as having their own personalities as well — with the conclusion that we can very credibly and reasonably argue that, when the ancient myths are describing the adventures and arguments of (for instance) the gods and goddesses of Olympus, they are in fact describing interactions which are characteristic of our own internal family of parts, familiar to every man and woman because we ourselves have some mixture of those same entities populating our own inner landscape!

Again, this assertion of mine is not intended to imply that Dr. Schwartz would agree with me here — but the insightful student of esoterism and ancient myth Alvin Boyd Kuhn (1880 – 1963) made a very similar assertion about the figures who populate the stories of the Bible when he stated in a 1936 lecture entitled *The Stable and the Manger* that:

> Bible stories are in no sense a record of what happened to
> a man or a people as historical occurrence. As such they
> would have little significance for mankind. They would be
> the experience of people not ourselves, and would not bear

a relation to our life. But they are a record, under pictorial forms, of that which is ever occurring as a reality of the present in all lives. They mean nothing as outward events; but they mean everything as picturizations of that which is our living experience at all times. The actors are not old kings, priests and warriors; the one actor in every portrayal, in every scene, is the human soul. the Bible is the drama of our history here and now; and it is not apprehended in its full force and applicability until every reader discerns himself [or herself] to be the central figure in it! the Bible is about the mystery of human life. Instead of relating to the incidents of a remote epoch in temporal history, it deals with the reality of the living present in the life of every soul on earth.[31]

Alvin Boyd Kuhn's assertion above is perfectly accurate, in my view — and I would add that my extensive research showing that the figures and events of the Bible stories are based on the stars adds conclusive proof that the Bible stories are "in no sense a record of . . . historical occurrence." The one vitally important element of understanding which can now be added to Kuhn's penetrating observation cited above is that, based upon the observations and insights of Richard Schwartz, we can now confidently perceive that each of us embodies a "multiplicity" rather than a "mono-mind" — we each have a full range of personalities within us, and thus when Kuhn states that the actors in the ancient stories (whether the stories of the Bible or the stories of Greek myth or of the ancient Sanskrit epics and Puranas and Vedas, or of the sacred traditions of any other culture, it does not matter) are "not old kings, priests and warriors" but rather that these stories are all about us, and that no reader has grasped the full force of the stories until he or she sees himself or herself to be the central figure in them, we can now expand Kuhn's statement to say "the actors in the ancient myths and scriptures are not old kings, priests and warriors — the actors dramatize the various parts and personalities which are found within every reader or listener, and we do not apprehend their full force and applicability until we see that these adventures and struggles are going on inside of each one of us!"

While the gods and goddesses are clearly portrayed as the source of our blessings and gifts in the ancient myths of the world, they are also shown to be in conflict with one another, as we have already seen in the story of the events leading up to the Trojan War, as well as during the entirety of the Trojan War itself when the various gods and goddesses arrange themselves on either side in the battle (and occasionally even switch sides in some cases). In a very similar way, Dr. Schwartz has found that these internal parts who each have their own gifts and resources to impart to us can and do become "polarized" and in conflict with one another, leading to divisions within the internal family. These divisions, I would add, very much mirror what we see dramatized in ancient myth.

Indeed, just as Dr. Schwartz calls his paradigm *Internal Family* Systems, because our various internal parts or personalities exhibit the same dynamics found within an *external* family, the gods and goddesses of ancient myth are often described as a family themselves! The gods and goddesses of Olympus, for example, are all part of the same extended family, with Zeus and Hera being the mother and father of most of them (although some, such as Athena and the twins Apollo and Artemis, are children of Zeus but not by Hera), while Poseidon and Hades are brothers of Zeus, all three of whom are children of the same father Kronos and his sister Rhea (Kronos and Rhea also being the father and mother of Hera, the wife of Zeus, as well).

In other words, while I am not suggesting that the gods of ancient Greece do *not* dwell in Olympus, I believe that a strong case can be made that they very much dwell *within* men and women as well — and that the same can be said of the figures described in all the other myths of the world (including, as Alvin Boyd Kuhn points out, the various characters we find in the stories of the Bible).

And, as Dr. Schwartz has found in his work, while they give us the gifts and resources that form the ingredients of our unique recipe of personal traits and strengths, they can also take on roles which seem to be counter-productive, and which lead to internal conflicts and power struggles. His early conversations with patients during "an outcome study with bulimic clients" (whose behaviors included alternating cycles of binging and purging) revealed that these clients were often very familiar with the different personalities arranged in their own internal families. He writes:

> I asked the clients to describe their parts, which they were able to do in great detail. Not only that, but they depicted how these parts interacted with each other and had relationships. Some fought, some formed alliances, and some protected others. Over time, it dawned on me that I was learning about a kind of inner system, not unlike the "external" families I was working with. Hence the name Internal Family Systems.[32]

Dr. Schwartz describes how he learned that it was fruitless to try to ignore difficult parts, or to somehow attempt to "banish" them. This approach, he found, only made things worse. It was only when he began to realize that the different parts act the way they do because they are carrying burdens or playing roles which *those parts feel they must carry or they must play for the survival of the entire internal system* that Dr. Schwartz began to find ways help clients to address those parts in order find out why they are doing what they are doing, and to heal the wounds that led to those polarizations and behaviors. He found that "each part — no matter how demonic seeming — has a secret, painful history to share of how it was forced into its role and came to carry burdens it doesn't like that continue to drive it."[33]

Think back now to the story of the events leading up to the disastrous conflict between the Achaeans and the Trojans upon the plains of Ilium in the myths of ancient Greece. It all started with the exclusion of Eris from the wedding feast of Thetis and Peleus over fears that inviting discord might damage the marriage (although if we go back even further, we might notice that the wedding of Thetis and Peleus itself came about because various gods were themselves afraid to marry her, having been told that her son would become greater than his own father).

Eris was thus, in a sense, *exiled* from the family of the gods — and she behaved in ways very much identical to the ways that Dr. Richard Schwartz has observed that exiled parts can behave, within the Internal Family Systems of men and women, over and over in thousands and thousands of instances. Trying to keep Eris out did not solve the problem of Discord at the wedding feast: in fact, it only made things worse! When turned away, Eris went to her sisters the Hesperides and brought back one of their golden apples, upon which she inscribed the provocative phrase which would end up creating a triangular quarrel between Hera, Athena and Aphrodite — again, in a pattern which can often be seen playing itself within our own internal landscapes, and which eventually led to even greater polarization as the Trojan War began and other gods and goddesses began to line up on either side of the conflict.

Here is Dr. Schwartz describing a conversation he had with an anorexic client whose internal parts had become polarized, to the point that one part was consistently keeping her from eating and threatening to kill her:

> I introduce myself and tell her that I'm good at helping people with the parts of them that make them not eat. I ask Margie where she finds that voice of anorexia in her body and how she feels toward it. She closes her eyes and says it's in her stomach, and she's angry at it. She says that it tells her that it's going to kill her and that there's nothing she can do about it. [...]
>
> In a calm, confident voice I tell Margie, "It makes sense that you're angry with the eating disorder part because its avowed purpose is to screw up your life or even kill you. But right now we just want to get to know it a little better, and it's hard to do that when you're so angry with it. We're not going to give it more power by doing that — just get to know more about why it wants to kill you. So see if the part of you that's so angry with it is willing to trust you and me for a few minutes. See if it's willing to relax and maybe watch as we try to get to know the eating disorder part." She says okay and when I ask her how she feels toward the eating disorder know, she says she's tired of battling with it. I have to ask that part to relax and step back too, and then another part that was very confused by the disorder. Remarkably for someone in her condition, each time she asks the part to step back, it does. Finally, in response

to my question of "how do you feel toward the eating disorder now?" she says in a compassionate voice, "Like, I want to help it."[34]

In this remarkable conversation, but one which is characteristic of the IFS approach and the paradigm of multiplicity, Dr. Schwartz encountered a number of polarized parts in his conversation with his suffering patient Margie, who at the time of this conversation had been struggling with anorexia for nineteen years and was wearing a feeding tube in her nose as she came into the office for therapy. Margie first described the part of her which, whenever she would begin to feel better about herself, would stop her from eating. This part frequently told Margie that it wanted to kill her and that she could do nothing to stop it.

Next, Dr. Schwartz encountered a different personality, another part, which was angry with the defiant, self-destructive part that was keeping Margie from eating and threatening to kill her. These two parts can be seen to be in a polarized relationship, according to the terminology developed by Dr. Schwartz for his IFS paradigm. To be "polarized" is to be "poles apart" and thus opposing one another, in a metaphor derived from the north and south poles of our Earth, or from the positive and negative poles of a magnet. The suicidal part preventing Margie from eating is actually trying to deal with psychic injury or trauma through the role that it has taken on within the internal family, while the angry part is similarly trying to "hold things together" but through different strategies and in conflict with the role that the suicidal part has taken on (hence, they are polarized, as if lining up on different sides of an internal battlefield).

We might wonder how a self-harming behavior as extreme as stopping us from eating, even potentially leading to self-inflicted death, can possibly be construed as "trying to hold the system together." The answer lies in the understanding that parts will take on these kinds of roles and exhibit such behaviors as a response to a deep wound or heartbreak that is so grievous that the parts believe it must not ever surface, because it is just too painful to experience. In the paradigm of Internal Family Systems, parts will take on various roles to try to keep such wounds from re-surfacing, including "manager" roles in which a part will (for instance) try to please others or gain worldly recognition, in order to prevent a deep childhood wound (such as a parent's telling the child, either verbally or non-verbally, that he or she would never be worth anything) from coming back onto the mental stage — to try to "lock out" that painful, toxic burden, in much the same way that the gods tried to lock Eris out from the feast.

But when the best proactive efforts of parts playing "manager" roles fails, and the trauma is triggered despite all the worldly achievements or people-pleasing behaviors performed by the managers, other parts will sail in to try to respond to the resurfacing of the trauma. These reactive parts will try to douse the resurfacing heartbreak through whatever means are necessary, even if those reactive behaviors cause chaos in the interim. Parts who feel forced to take on these reactive roles are labeled as "firefighters" in the Internal Family Systems paradigm, which is a very apt description in that firefighters will do whatever it takes to douse a fire in one building, even to the extent of spraying so much foam or water that it destroys everything in the building — because they have the larger mission of containing the fire and keeping it from burning down the neighborhood.

Firefighters, in other words, will cause temporary damage now and sort out the consequences later: anything to put out the fire that is raging. Similarly, parts playing a firefighter role will do whatever it takes to douse the flames of the re-triggered internal trauma, even if their firefighting efforts cause significant short-term damage. They view that as necessary, even if unpleasant. We are all familiar with the kinds of behaviors that firefighter parts can resort to: fits of rage, bouts of heavy drinking, binge-eating, and similar ways of "foaming down the house" to put out the fire. More extreme behaviors can include self-harming behaviors such as cutting. And, as Dr. Schwartz has explained, suicide is the ultimate form of self-destructive behavior, to which parts can resort when they see no other way to keep the traumatic feelings from resurfacing.

When Dr. Schwartz has Margie ask the angry part of her to step aside for a few minutes in order to be able to talk with the anorexia-inducing part and try to "get to know it," and find out why it wants to stop Margie from eating, the angry part complies with the request. As it moves aside, Margie voices the concern of yet another part — this time, a tired part who is worn out from the battle with the anorexia-inducing part. We are seeing yet another internal personality, but this one just wanting to give up, which is yet another survival strategy which our parts will sometimes exhibit, and which can manifest in the form of avoidance or deliberately not trying.

Again, Dr. Schwartz asks Margie if she can have this "exhausted" part step aside, and when she does so, we hear the voice of yet another part of Margie, one who is confused or bewildered by the behavior of the self-harming part that is stopping Margie from eating. The therapy session Schwartz is describing from his encounter with Margie reveals that we have numerous different personalities within us, and that these personalities can become embroiled in all kinds of internal dramas and soap operas, just as we see being dramatized for our benefit in the ancient myths of the world!

Finally, having asked each successive part to step aside temporarily in order to help have an inquisitive conversation with the anorexia-inducing part,

Dr. Schwartz hears a voice from Margie which does not express anger, nor exhaustion, nor bewilderment, but which instead exhibits compassion and the desire to help the wounded part who has taken up the role of stopping Margie from eating. This voice of compassion is coming from a different source, and one we will explore further in the following chapter. The main purpose of the above description from Dr. Schwartz's conversation with Margie is to illustrate the reality of the many fully-developed and virtually independent personalities which exist inside all of us, as well as some of the different roles that these parts can take on, roles which can sometimes become extreme and even self-destructive.

The polarization described by Dr. Richard Schwartz and other practitioners, and which we see exhibited in this encounter with Margie and her parts, is dramatized in the myths, and bears a striking resemblance to the stories of the exclusion of Eris and the subsequent quarrels leading to the Judgement of Paris and ultimately to the Trojan War. It is noteworthy that in the same essay in which he describes this session with Margie, Dr. Schwartz states (describing parts who are playing roles that are self-destructive or otherwise unwelcome): "there's no shortcut around our inner barbarians — those unwelcome parts of ourselves, such as hatred, rage, suicidal despair, fear, addictive need (for drugs, food, sex), racism and other prejudice, greed, as well as the somewhat less heinous feelings of ennui, guilt, depression, anxiety, self-righteousness, and self-loathing. The lesson I've repeatedly learned over the years is that we must learn to listen to and ultimately embrace these unwelcome parts."[35]

An important point to understand regarding parts who have taken on distasteful roles or who exhibit unwelcome behaviors, such as those listed by Dr. Schwartz in the above statement, is that these personalities within us *are not their roles*: they *take on* these roles or exhibit these behaviors because they are trying to deal with psychological injuries of some kind, and generally in order to keep that hurt *locked up* and *buried away*, out of sight and out of mind. Our different parts themselves are benevolent and well-intentioned, and as Dr. Schwartz says in a statement cited earlier, "all of our parts have valuable qualities and resources to give us."

Again, the same can be said of the gods and goddesses described in the ancient myths given to all the cultures of the world. The gods and goddesses all demonstrate valuable qualities, in fact indispensable qualities, and they all have resources to give to us. But, as we see dramatized in the myths, they have what might be termed their "shadow sides" as well.

A helpful example can readily be seen by looking at the nature of the powerful god Zeus, the ruler of Olympus and king of the gods of ancient Greece. Zeus is a benevolent god, and our word "jovial" comes from his name among the Latins: Jove (who also called him Jupiter, a name which may be derived from "Zeus the Father," *Zeus Pater*, as the linguistic sounds for "Z" and "J" are related). Zeus or Jove or Jupiter is a jovial god, and one who loves a good feast and a jolly party — but he is also a god with a short temper and a powerful rage, the god of thunder and lightning and the mighty storm.

The Orphic Hymns contain at least three different hymns explicitly devoted to Zeus, praising him for his greatness and acknowledging him as the father of all, and asking him for his blessings, including health, riches, victory, cheerful thoughts, and "glory without blame."[36] Each, however, also mentions the god's fearful power, and his terrifying anger. Hymn 20 addresses him as "O horrid [horror-inducing], O wrathful and pure, O invincible god, lord of lightning."[37]

Other sky- and thunder-gods around the world, including both Thor and the God of the Bible (Jah or Jehovah or YHWH, whose sacred name has clear linguistic parallels to the name of Jove or Jupiter or Zeus Pater), can be clearly seen to exhibit the same pattern of general benevolence coupled with sudden wrathfulness and terrifying anger. The point being illustrated is that the gods described in the ancient myths and scriptures given to humanity can be seen to simultaneously embody what we might call "shadow and light" sides, capable of acting beneficially but also in ways that might be seen as more "unwelcome."

In other words, they are portrayed in myth as acting in ways that very much parallel what Dr. Richard Schwartz has found to be true of the way our own internal "multiple personalities" or parts act as well.

Many more examples could be offered from Greek myth alone, supported by verses in the Orphic Hymns which is a convenient source of ancient expression regarding the well-known aspects of the ancient deities, and which can also be supported by examples from other textual records describing the gods and their characteristics and actions. Of the goddess Persephone, who is both the bringer of Spring and the Queen of the Underworld, the Orphic Hymns say: "O Persephone, You nourish all, always, and kill them too."[38] Of the god Pan, the pastoral god of shepherds and springs and woodlands, it is said, "On the boundless earth, you offer nourishment to mankind," but also, "You induce fantasies of dread into the minds of mortals."[39] Of Hermes, messenger of Zeus, it is noted that he is the god of words, which can carry blessings to others and be used to soothe conflict and bring about peace, but which can also wound like a knife, or be used for the purposes of deceit.[40]

As we have already seen, the gods live *in us* and express themselves *through us* — and thus it is not inaccurate to understand that our own individual makeup will naturally tend to have more or less influence of each of the various gods and goddesses, and that, just as Dr. Schwartz has described regarding the concept of our internal family of parts, these gods inside both bestow positive gifts upon our lives but can also exhibit what we might see as the "shadow sides" of their nature.

If we are driving down the road, for example, and another driver cuts in front of us without warning and in violation of the established rules governing "right-of-way," and we feel ourselves filling with rage or even verbally cursing the other driver, perhaps even going so far as feeling urges to actually fight, we might consider that this response could actually be appropriate if we should ever be faced with a situation in which we had to physically defend our own person or others around us. If we woke up in the middle of the night and a violent intruder had broken into our home, such a flood of violent energy might not be at all inappropriate, especially if we had to defend others in our household, such as our children.

If we were to ask which god would be most associated with these aspects of our personality, among the pantheon of the myths of Greece it might be the god Ares, the violent god of war. If we have been blessed with resources given by Ares, we might be find such gifts to be extremely beneficial in competitive endeavors, as well as in the less-common situation in which we actually do need to rise to the act of physical conflict or self-defense. The Orphic Hymn dedicated to Ares begins by describing the god as, "Unbreakable, strong-spirited, mighty, [. . .] indomitable," all of which are characteristics we might well desire for ourselves. But the hymn goes on to describe Ares as "ever bespattered with blood" and always finding joy in killing and violence.[41]

We can recognize that the resources associated with Ares including strength of will and indomitable spirit, as well as the use of sudden physical force or even violence, can be appropriate or justified in some situations, but inappropriate and unwelcome in others. We don't want to get rid of (or altogether banish) that aspect of who we are, no matter how much or how little of the "gifts of Ares" we possess. In fact, we cannot get rid of our parts even if we wanted to (and we need those resources brought to us by every member of our team, or our internal family). But we want those parts of who we are to behave in ways that are welcome and appropriate, and not unwelcome and potentially harmful.

The concluding verses of the Hymn to Ares beseech the god to "Stay the rage, stay the strife," and to yield to the wishes of Kypris (meaning the goddess Aphrodite, born on Cyprus), and the yearning for "youth-bringing peace, bliss-bringing peace."[42] We see here evidence of ancient understanding for a connection between Ares and Aphrodite, which is also dramatized in both the Iliad and the Odyssey, and a plea which basically indicates that the powers of Ares can be turned towards the promotion of peace and bliss and, in fact, love.

All of the gods have something positive to offer us, resources we need in this life — but they can take on unwelcome roles, and plunge into discord and strife, as we have seen in the story of the genesis of the Trojan War. When taking stock of our own internal families, this principle of "shadow sides" can be very helpful to us in understanding the way that necessary gifts and strengths can be twisted into something harmful and negative. From this understanding, we can then ask how those necessary and helpful resources could regain their positive roles, if their strengths could be turned in the proper direction, just as the Hymn to Ares indicates.

And according to the Iliad, Eris is the sister and companion of Ares. The poem describes her as starting out "a very small thing at first," but growing until she strides the earth with her head striking the heavens.[43] The Iliad goes on, a few lines later, to say that she sows strife and discord equally between both sides (in this instance, meaning between the Achaeans and the Trojans alike), "destructive to all."[44]

Internally, these buried seeds of Discord will cause the gods within to polarize, just as we saw illustrated in the conversation that Richard Schwartz had with a woman suffering from anorexia, in which one voice was declaring that it would stop her from eating, while another part is angry with the one who is using those tactics, and yet another is expressing exhaustion and saying she is tired of battling with that anorexic part. The myths are dramatizing what takes place within us when parts are forced into roles that they may not wish to play, forced to take on jobs that they might rather not have chosen, but which they feel that they must take on, out of necessity, in order to hold the entire system together (or, said another way, for the good of the entire inner family).

But the myths show us that this "Discord among the gods" can be placated and resolved — even as Dr. Schwartz describes seeing during his interactions with so many thousands of men and women whose internal personalities have been enabled to move out of unwelcome roles and into a role in which they can express their strengths in a more positive way. That kind of harmony cannot be reached, however, until that source of Discord can be identified — and often that source has been buried deep and forgotten (deliberately forgotten, as a defense mechanism).

The myths dramatize this need to discover the source that is causing disharmony, and no one explains this fact better perhaps than mystic philosopher

Peter Kingsley, using as an example an event found at the beginning of the text of the Iliad. In a lecture included in a collection of talks entitled *The Elders*, Kingsley says:

> Prophecy is not about the future. Prophets don't talk about the future. What they do is: they talk about the past -- which has been hidden. Things which have happened -- that have been *covered over*, and no longer clear. That is what the real prophets do: they speak about the past, but the past that has been forgotten.

> And you can see this if you look: you can see, say, with Empedocles -- this man I'm so connected with. As a prophet, he tries to point out to people what they have forgotten, what has gone wrong, what is missing -- why they don't function in the world anymore, why there is so much suffering, disease, disharmony, misery: because we've forgotten our divine source. He traces it all back.

> And you can see it also at the very beginning of Homer's Iliad, when there is a whole plague. The soldiers are devastated, by sickness and plague. They're suffering; they're dying. And what happens, in this case? They find a prophet, and they ask him what's going wrong. And he says: "Apollo -- these are the arrows of Apollo. He's shot these arrows of plague, into the troops, because you did something wrong, you offended

Apollo." And then it all becomes very simple. Because you see, once you know what's wrong, then you can sort it out -- you can make amends. It's very, very precise. That is what prophecy is.

And if you look at this process -- I've just said a little about it -- if you look at this *real* process of prophecy, you see that this is -- or this used to be -- the *corrective element* in human life. This is what brought people back into connection with the divine.[45]

There is a wealth of wisdom in the above passage regarding the causes of "suffering, disease, disharmony, misery." Peter Kingsley points to the beginning of the Iliad, in which the god Apollo has been angered by the disrespectful treatment of Agamemnon towards Chryses, a priest of Apollo, whose daughter Chryseis has been taken as a war-trophy by Agamemnon. In the very first lines of the epic poem, Chryses approaches Agamemnon, bearing priceless treasures with which to ransom his captured daughter, and begging Agamemnon to give Chryseis her freedom, and in doing so also to honor Apollo, whom Chryses serves.

Although the poem notes that all the Achaean warriors shouted their assent to this impassioned request and urge the king to take the bountiful ransom and let the girl go, Agamemnon responds harshly and insultingly to the heartbroken father, telling the old priest to never let himself be caught lurking around the camp of the Greek warriors again, and declaring that the girl will sooner grow to old age far from home as a servant in the bedroom of Agamemnon before she is ever given her liberty. As Chryses retreats in fear from the threats of the king, he implores Apollo to make the followers of Agamemnon pay — and the poem describes the sickness and death that ensue when Apollo releases his plague-bearing arrows among the camp of the Achaeans.

Ultimately, Agamemnon relents and allows Chryseis to return to her father in order to appease the god and stop the invisible onslaught. But the prideful king then demands that Achilles turn over Briseis, the young woman whom Achilles took during the same raid in which Chryseis was captured and awarded to Agamemnon, as a replacement. What kind of insecurity or deep feeling of inadequacy is Agamemnon trying to compensate for and cover up with these insulting and petty actions and words? As the most powerful king leading the various contingents of warriors against the walls of Troy, Agamemnon can clearly get whatever he wants, but instead of acting with graciousness and compassion for others, he demeans himself and introduces all kinds of disharmony among his own ranks — even inviting the wrath of Apollo which leads to disease and death among those who don't seem to deserve it, and who were not responsible for Agamemnon's insulting behavior (in fact, the poem tells us that they urged the king to give the girl back to her father).

As Peter Kingsley's explication of this incident teaches us, the disease being sent by Apollo does not stop until the source of the disharmony is pinpointed. In the Iliad, the goddess Hera, concerned about the mounting losses of Achaean warriors under the arrows of Apollo, inspires Achilles to seek out the augur or seer Calchas, to find out how they have angered the god so that they can correct the problem.

As Peter Kingsley points out, the prophet Calchas here is not divining the future: he is being called upon to divine the past — "things which have happened" but which "have been covered over." Sources of our present disharmony are found in the past: "the past which has been forgotten." And, just as with the case of the woman Dr. Schwartz calls Margie, deep buried issues can lead to polarization which actually manifest in physical illness, because our internal parts (the gods within) can actually "pull levers" which impact different parts of our body and even our physical health, in their efforts to get our attention.

The god Apollo is the god of music, and also the god of health — but in what we might call the "shadow" side of these gifts, the Iliad shows him sending plague-filled arrows when the god is angered by the insulting and disrespectful behavior of Agamemnon (behavior which, as noted above, almost certainly arises from some deep issue in Agamemnon's own personal history and which Agamemnon is trying to "cover over" with his inflexible attempts to avoid anything which he sees as causing himself to lose face in any way). When our internal divine family becomes polarized, we see the unwelcome sides of the very gods who could also be the source of blessing.

But, as Peter Kingsley explains and as the events of the first section of the Iliad dramatize for our understanding, "once you know what's wrong, then you can sort it out — you can make amends." It requires a proper understanding of our own past — and an identification of what aspects of our past are causing the present disharmony and discord. As American author William Faulkner (1897 – 1962) famously wrote, "The past is never dead. It's not even past."[46] That past is still within us, and polarizations of the gods within will not be restored to harmony until we recognize and sort out those sources of discord.

And, as Peter Kingsley asserts towards the end of the passage cited, the recovery requires coming back into "connection with the divine."

But in this physical world, and in this modern age, do we have any way of recovering connection with the divine?

The ancient wisdom given to us in the sacred myths of the world show us quite positively that we do.

Chapter Three

The Golden Age

T he plague was raging among the Achaean warriors camped out along the line of their ships, pulled up onto the beaches of the land of Troy. Columns of smoke rose from funeral pyres bearing the bodies of the dead, who had succumbed to the dreaded arrows of Apollo. For nine days, the disease had continued to mount like a rising tide, but on the tenth — spurred by the inspiration of the goddess Hera, who had become increasingly concerned at the swelling death toll — the great warrior Achilles called for an assembly of all the people.

Addressing Agamemnon directly, Achilles declared that it was time for those who had not already been afflicted with the disease to admit defeat and sail away immediately, if indeed they could escape. Either that, he said, or they had better find "some prophet, some priest, or even one who is informed by dreams (for dream also is from Jove)," to find out how they had offended Apollo.[47]

In the book of Genesis, Joseph the son of Jacob was similarly informed of the will of the divine through dreams. His dream of being in the field at harvest with his brothers when suddenly his sheaf of wheat stood up taller than those of his brothers, at which time all their sheaves bowed down to

Joseph's sheaf, did not at all endear him to the other sons of Jacob, nearly all of whom were older than Joseph (except for Benjamin, the youngest of them all and the only other son of Jacob by Rachel, his favorite wife). Joseph was Jacob's favorite, a fact which was not a secret and which also did not endear Joseph to his older eleven brothers. And when Joseph related another dream, in which he said he saw the Sun and the Moon along with eleven stars bowing down before himself (Joseph), his brothers hated him even more (Genesis 37: 5 – 11).

Soon after, while the older eleven brothers were tending the family flocks grazing in the fields north of Shechem, Jacob sent Joseph (who was seventeen years old at the start of the chapter in which these events are related, and thus is probably still seventeen at the time or perhaps eighteen) to check on them. Joseph had already earned the resentment of his brothers by bringing back an unfavorable report of their actions while grazing the flocks earlier in the text, in addition to his description of the two dreams mentioned above, and when the older brothers saw Joseph coming, they said to one another, "O look: here comes this master of dreams" — "Let's kill him and throw his body into a pit, and then we'll see whether his dreams come true or not!" (Genesis 37: 12 – 20)

Joseph's life was spared by the intervention of the firstborn of Jacob's sons, Reuben, who prevailed upon them to throw Joseph down into a pit and leave him there alive, with Reuben planning to come back and rescue Joseph later. Reuben never got the chance to pull Joseph back out, however, because before he could do so, the other brothers saw a caravan of Midianites passing by, and sold Joseph to them for twenty pieces of silver (as an aside, the text alternates between calling these merchants "Midianites" and "Ishmaelites," once referring to them by both names in the same sentence, which is somewhat problematic to literalist interpreters, because Ishmaelites are descended from Ishmael, the son of Abraham by Hagar the handmaid of Sarai or Sarah, while Midianites are descended from Midian, a later son of Abraham by a concubine named Keturah, with whom Abraham bears additional children after the death of Sarah — but some literalist scholars overcome this difficulty by asserting that Keturah must be another name for Hagar)(Genesis 27: 25 – 28).

The text tells us that the Midianites eventually sell Joseph to Potiphar, the captain of the guard of the Pharaoh of Egypt, where Joseph ends up in prison after being falsely accused of rape by Potiphar's wife. After languishing in prison, Joseph's demonstrated ability to interpret the will of heaven through dreams eventually brings the young man to the attention of the Pharaoh, who has been having troubling dreams which none of Pharaoh's magicians and wise men can interpret (Genesis 40 and Genesis 41: 1 – 36).

Joseph's ability to understand the cryptic symbolism of dreams, an ability which Joseph himself emphasizes does not come from within him but only from the divine source — from God — enables him to advise Pharaoh about the proper course of action to take to avert disaster in an upcoming period of famine. Joseph's judgement and demonstrated ability to see the right path result in his eventual elevation by the age of thirty to a position of absolute authority over the entire kingdom, second only to Pharaoh himself (Genesis 41: 37 – 57).

Eventually, the famine brings his brothers to Egypt to seek grain in order to save their own lives and that of their mother and father — and Joseph has them ushered into his presence while he decides their fate, although they do not recognize Joseph in this high-ranking leader of all Egypt (Joseph, of course, recognizes *them*). After some episodes in which he hides his identity and deals harshly with them, each time having to break away and regain his composure because he is overcome with tears, Joseph eventually can restrain his emotion no further, because (as the text tells us) he is so deeply filled with compassion for them (Genesis 43 – 45).

I have shown conclusively that the stories of the Bible — including the stories surrounding Jacob and his children (as well as the stories surrounding the life of Jacob's parents Isaac and Rebekah, and those surrounding Isaac's parents Abraham and Sarah, and so on throughout Genesis and then all the way through the Old and New Testaments), and including of course the story of Joseph and all of the above-cited episodes — are based on celestial *metaphor*, and I would argue that they are almost certainly *entirely* metaphorical, and not historical whatsoever.

Absolutely overwhelming evidence shows that the identities of the children of Jacob are associated with the constellations of the zodiac (the sons of Jacob are more commonly called the "children of Israel," because Jacob's name was changed to Israel following his encounter with a divine messenger at the ford Jabbok, also called Peniel, recounted in Genesis 32, an encounter which itself can be shown to be based on celestial metaphor, as I demonstrate in my course entitled *The Celestial Bible Tour*).

While those from cultures strongly influenced by centuries of Biblical literalism (as well as those who themselves continue to hold a literalist position) commonly ask me if it is not possible that these stories are both demonstrably celestial but also at the same time historical, such an argument is very difficult to maintain, if the primary "evidence" for their historicity is drawn from texts which (like the rest of the world's ancient myths, scriptures, and sacred stories) can be shown to be celestial and metaphorical — and which, as we will see, are using the same over-arching system of metaphor to advance very much the same esoteric message which is being advanced in the Biblical stories.

Further, one might ask why we should somehow assume that the Biblical stories (based on celestial metaphor as they demonstrably are) would *also* be historical, while no such consideration is given to the mythical figures of *other* cultures. If one wishes to argue that Moses or Samson (who can be conclusively shown to be celestial and related directly to specific constellations) might also somehow be based on historical figures, wouldn't the same question be appropriate for mythical figures from other cultures, such as Hercules of ancient Rome, or Hunahpu and Xbalanque of the Maya Popol Vuh, or Maui of the Polynesian cultures of the islands of the vast Pacific?

Yet further, if stories such as Joseph being sold into slavery by his brothers, or Moses extending his staff as God parts the Red Sea, *can be shown* to correspond to specific constellations in the sky (which they can) and *yet are also* historical events which took place in the lives of actual individual persons, then what does that have to say about individual "free will" and volition? Was Moses *foreordained* to hold out his staff towards the Red Sea at some point in his life, an action *he* could not possibly refuse or resist, in order to *match up with the stars* of the constellation Ophiuchus, which can be seen across many cultures to appear as figures who carry either a staff or a rod or a long spear, and which can be seen to be pointing that spear towards the "Dark Rift" which leads across the band of the Milky Way, exactly as God's parting of the Red Sea opens a path for the children of Israel to walk across "on dry ground"?

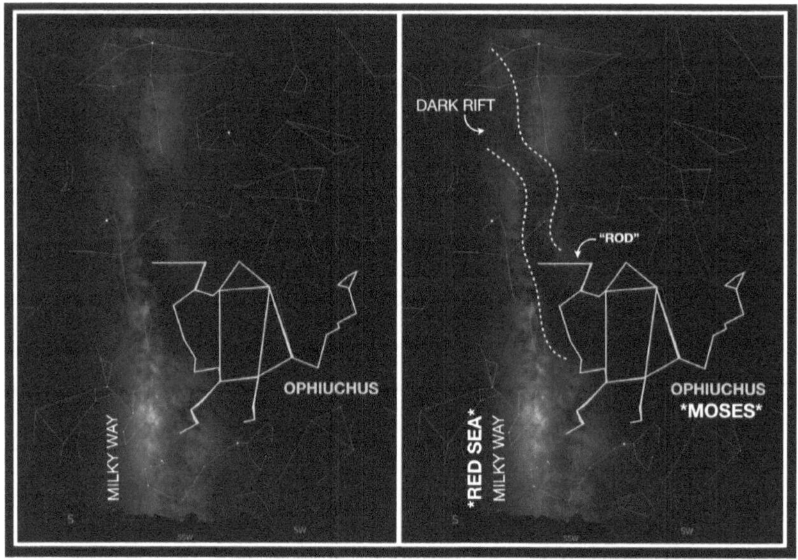

It would seem that the conclusion that the Biblical stories (in common with the ancient myths of other cultures around the globe) are entirely metaphorical is much more tenable than the hypothesis that the Bible stories are somehow *both* an account of literal, terrestrial historical events and *simultaneously* based upon celestial metaphor. In any case, the burden of proof is upon those who wish to assert that the Bible stories are somehow also literal history: it can be shown beyond any shadow of doubt that they are celestial metaphor.

But if the story of Joseph (along with other stories in the Bible, and myths from virtually every other culture around the world) is based on celestial metaphor, what is that metaphor supposed to signify? What could it possibly be trying to tell us?

Recall in the previous chapter entitled "Discord" that Dr. Richard Schwartz describes a conversation he had with a woman suffering from anorexia. His patient, Margie, described a part of her who was telling

Margie it was going to kill her by stopping her from eating, and who added that there was nothing she could do about it.

Recall that when Margie revealed this to him, Dr. Schwartz then asked how Margie felt about that defiantly self-destructive (potentially lethally self-destructive) part, and Margie replied that she was angry at the anorexic part — and understandably so. However, at that point, Dr. Schwartz asked the angry part of Margie if it would please step aside, in order to see if he and Margie could talk to that anorexic part in order to perhaps learn more about its motives in taking on such a dangerously unwelcome role. Note that before he made that request, he honored the part of Margie who was angry at the anorexic part, saying that it was certainly understandable to be angry at the anorexic part.

When Margie told Dr. Schwartz that the angry part had stepped aside in order to let them try to talk with the anorexic part, Dr. Schwartz asked Margie again how she felt about the anorexic part now — and received the answer that she felt "tired of battling with it." Dr. Schwartz again asked this part to step aside (after, I'm sure, honoring that part for the role it had been playing in the internal drama, and asking it to trust him and Margie enough to give some space in order to converse with the dangerous anorexic part).

As he describes, Dr. Schwartz then asked Margie the same question yet again, and yet again received an answer from a part who said that it was confused by the whole situation, and again Dr. Schwartz asked this part if it would trust them enough to just step aside for a moment and give them access to have a conversation with the anorexia-inducing part. Once again, this confused part acceded to the request and gave Margie and Dr. Schwartz space to proceed.

Dr. Schwartz said he asked Margie again how she felt about the anorexic part, and Margie then replied: "Like, I want to help it."

This was the moment Dr. Schwartz was waiting for. After Margie says this, Dr. Schwartz writes: "The moment in a session when a client suddenly has access to some degree of Self always gives me goose bumps."[48]

When he hears Margie express compassion for the part of her who has taken on the unwelcome role of inducing anorexia and declaring its intent to kill her no matter what she tries to do to stop it, Dr. Schwartz knows he is hearing Margie's deeper Self, her authentic Self, speaking — as opposed to another part who is polarized in some way with the anorexic part. The other voices he heard previously expressed anger, exhaustion, and confusion — but after asking each of these parts to step aside for a few minutes, Dr. Schwartz and Margie finally arrive at a different voice, one who expresses the desire to help the anorexia-inducing part. From this expression of compassion Dr. Schwartz was able to perceive the arrival of Self.

In his book *No Bad Parts*, Dr. Schwartz explains that what he has come to call the Self is in everybody, consistently demonstrating a set of characteristics which can be recognized to distinguish Self from the various parts. Over the course of his years of interaction with clients, he found that Self would arise when the various other parts, who were playing different roles in their efforts to "hold the system together," could be asked to step back and take a short break from their accustomed roles. Schwartz writes:

> The simple act of getting these other parts to open more
> space inside seemed to release someone who had curiosity

but who was also calm and confident relative to the critic. When my clients were in this place, the dialogue would go well. The critic would drop its guard and tell its secret history and the client would have compassion for it and we would learn about what it protected, and so on. Client after client, the same mindfully curious, calm, confident, and often even compassionate part would pop up out of the blue and that part seemed to know how to relate internally in a healing way. And when they were in that state, I'd ask clients, "Now, what part of you is that?" and they'd say, "That's not a part like these others, that's more myself," or "That's more my core" or "That's who I really am."[49]

Contrary to what he had been taught in all of his formal psychology training, Dr. Schwartz discovered over time that this calm and confident and compassionate Self was present in men and women no matter what kind of childhood they had experienced, even in men and women who had experienced horrible abuse and trauma. He says:

> After thousands of hours of doing this work, I can say with certainty that the Self is in everybody. Furthermore, the Self cannot be damaged, the Self doesn't have to develop, and the Self possesses its own wisdom about how to heal internal as well as external relationships.[50]

This Self can be suppressed and buried by the other parts, as a result of psychological injury (including attachment injury, which results from a sense of betrayal or rejection from someone to whom we are very attached, such as a parent) and trauma. But, as Dr. Schwartz asserts in the sentences cited above, Self is indestructible and cannot be damaged, let alone destroyed or eliminated. Self is waiting just beneath the surface, and Self instinctively knows how to heal the various parts, even highly polarized parts, and help them come back into harmony, shed unwelcome roles, and take on more positive roles which allow their various gifts and resources to be used in positive ways.

Over time, as he encountered this intrinsic and universally-available deeper Self in client after client, Dr. Schwartz began to catalogue the properties of Self which he saw being exhibited over and over when Self rose to the surface. He has come up with a list of characteristics which begin with the letter "c" in English, and which he finds to be intrinsic to Self across men and women of all backgrounds and all kinds of different childhoods and personal experiences.

The characteristics of Self in this list are known as the "Eight C's" in Schwartz's Internal Family Systems paradigm of therapy, and they are: Compassion, Curiosity, Clarity, Creativity, Confidence, Courage, Connectedness, and Calm. He later added another list of characteristics which he has observed to describe Self in men and women, the "Five P's" of Patience, Persistence, Presence, Perspective, and Playfulness.

Recall that when Dr. Schwartz was interviewing Margie, he immediately knew when he was hearing a part who was not Self, because when we hear a part expressing anger, exhaustion, or bewilderment, those are not characteristics of Self. Self inherently expresses compassion and patience rather than anger, persistence and confidence rather than exhaustion, and in contrast to confusion, Self is characterized by clarity and an amazing ability to know what to do in any situation.

Now consider the story of Joseph and his brothers from the book of Genesis. His brothers turn against him when he is still very young, and eventually they throw him down into a pit. In fact, there is some degree of polarization among his different brothers, in that some of them want to kill Joseph, while at least one of the brothers (Reuben) advises against killing Joseph but instead advises throwing him into the pit, with a plan to come back later and rescue his brother.

Despite this incident, and despite later being sold into slavery and ending up in a far-off land, where he is then falsely accused of rape and thrown into prison for years, Joseph has an inherent connection to the divine, and an ability to interpret dreams. He exhibits such clarity of vision, in fact, that he saves the land of Egypt from famine, when he interprets the dream of the Pharaoh and councils the leaders of the country to store up grain during the upcoming seven years of abundant harvests, in order to prepare for the subsequent years of failed harvests.

When his brothers come to see him — the very brothers who had plotted to kill him, and who had thrown Joseph down into a pit, and later sold the boy to the caravan of Midianites — Joseph is actually overcome with compassion, saving them and restoring their relationship with him by exhibiting compassionate leadership which they did not expect.

In short, the story of Joseph dramatically illustrates aspects of Self, as well as the turmoil of the often-polarized landscape of our internal parts (our internal family). Joseph's brothers can be seen as representative of our various parts, and Joseph himself exhibits the characteristics of Self — including the fact that Self is often suppressed and "buried" by the various parts, as well as the fact that Self is indestructible and "cannot be damaged" (an aspect of Self which is dramatized again and again in the ancient myths of cultures around the Earth). Joseph exhibits the characteristics that Dr. Schwartz has found to be inherent aspects of Self over the course of thousands of client interactions, including *clarity* (Joseph knows what to do in order to save Egypt) and *compassion*.

In short, the ancient story of Joseph and his brothers is an almost perfect metaphor dramatizing our own inner landscape, complete with a quarrelsome internal family, polarization, suppression of Self, and the potential for the recovery of Self and the healing of polarization and past injuries and trauma.

Now, examine the painting below entitled *Joseph Reveals his Dream to his Brethren*, by James Jacques Joseph Tissot (1836 – 1902):

In this remarkable piece of art, Joseph is seated upon a hillock while his brothers sit or loll in the grass of the fields below and around him. Some of the brothers express boredom, others show resentment and perhaps anger. We know from the story itself that some of them would be thinking to themselves, "I am going to kill him." Joseph appears to be lecturing his older brothers while they are cooking their lunch — perhaps Tissot is showing the scene of the Joseph's arrival among his brothers at Dothan north of Shechem, not long before they decide to throw him into a pit and later sell him to the Midianites.

Below is an image of the night sky, centered on the path of the ecliptic and its background constellations, which are known as the zodiac constellations:

The "ecliptic" is the term given to the path of the sun across the sky, which itself is determined by the orbital plane between our planet and the sun. As our planet turns on its axis, the sun will cross the sky from east to west, and during the course of the year as the angle of our axial tilt changes in relation to the sun, the path of the sun across the sky will creep further towards the north (as the North Pole of our planet is tilted more towards the sun) and then further towards the south (as the South Pole of our planet is tilted more towards the sun). The paths of the moon and all of our solar system's planets will also likewise cut across our sky along paths which are fairly close to the line of the ecliptic, since all of these bodies are generally orbiting along the same plane, with some different inclinations from one sphere to the next.

In the image above, we see the zodiac constellations through which that ecliptic passes, arrayed across the entire sky. The path of the sun throughout the year would travel from right to left as we see it depicted here, such that after passing through the constellation of Taurus (on the right edge of the illustration) the sun would then proceed to Gemini and then Cancer and so on, reaching Aries (on the left of the illustration) after passing through Pisces. After traveling through Aries, the sun (or any of the planets) would then proceed into Taurus again, as the illustration here is a kind of "spread out" fisheye-lens picture of the dome of the heavens, which I made using Stellarium.

Note that in addition to the familiar twelve zodiac constellations (Aries, Taurus, Gemini, Cancer, Leo, Virgo, Libra, Scorpio, Sagittarius, Capricorn, Aquarius, and Pisces) there is one other constellation through which the ecliptic path of the sun, moon and planets will pass — the constellation Ophiuchus, one "foot" of whom appears to "dip down" into the path of the ecliptic and across which the sun will travel during its annual journey around the zodiac.

Ophiuchus itself resembles a mound or a hill or even a mountain — and the constellation plays that role in many ancient myths from around the world, as I have demonstrated in previous volumes including *The Ancient World-Wide System*. Note also that, as we saw with the previous brief discussion of the identity of Moses and his staff, the band of the Milky Way at its widest and brightest rises directly adjacent to the standing figure of Ophiuchus, passing first in between Scorpio and Sagittarius (and covering most of the eastern part of the constellation Scorpio) before proceeding northwards (upwards in the diagram) past Ophiuchus.

Now consider again the painting by James Tissot depicting Joseph seated upon a mound above his other brothers — brothers who can confidently and beyond any argument be identified with the twelve constellations of the zodiac, as the "blessing of Jacob" recited in the text of Genesis 49 makes clear. Tissot has depicted the smoke from the cooking-fire rising up to the left of Joseph — just as the Milky Way rises up along the entire eastern side of Ophiuchus in the sky (the left side of Ophiuchus, if we are in the northern hemisphere facing south, with the "feet" of Ophiuchus facing "down" to the horizon). The image below juxtaposes Tissot's painting with the star chart, in what might be called *Joseph and his Brothers compared with Ophiuchus and the Zodiac*:

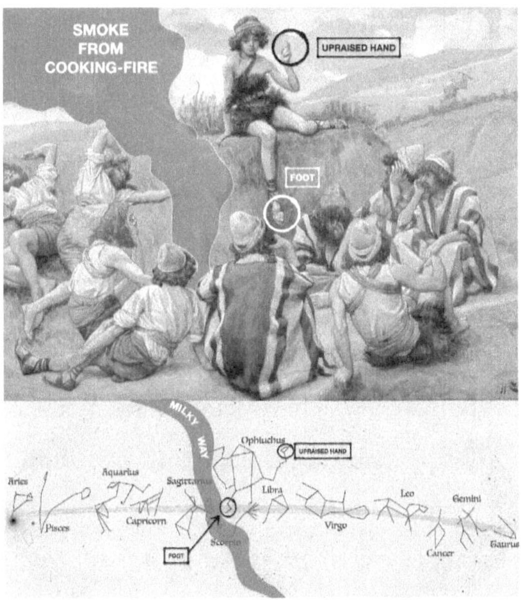

The positioning of Joseph in the location of Ophiuchus cannot be merely accidental or coincidental in this painting. Not only is Joseph positioned upon a mound (with Ophiuchus in myth often being associated with mounds, mountains, and even ant-hills as I have demonstrated in other books) and not only is Joseph positioned alongside the rising smoke from the fire in the very same position that the constellation Ophiuchus is positioned relative to the Milky Way (with the Milky Way in myth often being associated with pillars of fire and columns of smoke, and with Tissot's depiction of the fire in the painting bearing a striking resemblance to the shape and outline of the Milky Way itself), but Tissot has also depicted one of Joseph's feet dangling down into the "plane of the ecliptic" that is defined by the circle of his zodiacal brothers! Indeed, the foot of Joseph which dips down into the circle of his brethren is the foot closest to the rising smoke, just as we can clearly seen in the outline of Ophiuchus in the heavens, where it is the easternmost foot of the constellation, which is to say the foot of the constellation closest to the Milky Way (the foot on the left as we face the diagram above) which dips down into the ecliptic plane and is crossed by the path of the sun!

Just in case we need any additional clues, Tissot has also depicted Joseph in the painting with one hand upraised, in the same position that we find the "serpent's head" of Ophiuchus on the west side of the constellation (the side further from the Milky Way, which is the side opposite the foot which dips down into the ecliptic path, and the right side of the constellation as seen in the diagram above). These details leave us absolutely no doubt whatsoever that Tissot's painting is depicting Joseph in the position of Ophiuchus, with Joseph's brothers as the zodiac constellations, although Tissot does not depict all twelve brothers (he doesn't have to: the symbology is undeniable as painted).

How these celestial conventions were passed down among artists for centuries (and indeed for millennia) around the world is a fascinating question, and one about which we can only speculate at this point, but there is no doubt that Tissot somehow decided to depict Joseph in the position of Ophiuchus in the painting of Joseph revealing his dreams to his brethren. And, as I have argued above, there should also be no doubt that the story of Joseph dramatizes almost perfectly the struggles which take place within our own internal landscape as discovered by Dr. Richard Schwartz over the course of all those many thousands of client or patient interactions, in which the multiple "parts" of our internal family become polarized and suppress our authentic Self, attempting to banish or to bury the Self, but Self is indestructible and can be restored and in doing so heal the old wounds and restore harmony within the internal system, exhibiting clarity and compassion and the other attractive traits which are inherent to Self no matter what trauma has taken place in the past.

I have shown in previous books, including 2019's *Ancient World-Wide System* and 2020's *Myth and Trauma* that figure in myth who are representative of this higher Self almost invariably appear as figures associated with the constellation Ophiuchus. At the time that I wrote and published those previous books, however, I was not even aware of the existence of Dr. Schwartz and the Internal Family System paradigm which he had discovered over the course of his research and analysis of what he saw taking place in the lives of his clients.

I *was* at the time of writing *Myth and Trauma* aware of the work of Dr. Gabor Maté, whose research and client work makes clear that psychological trauma results in disconnection from and suppression of the Self, often without our even realizing that we have become disconnected from Self and that we have suppressed our own Self. Therefore, because Ophiuchus is the "forgotten" or "excluded" constellation — in that it does have a connection with the ecliptic plane which defines the constellations included in the zodiac, and yet Ophiuchus itself is not included in the zodiac along with the other constellations of Aries, Taurus, Gemini, Cancer, Leo, Virgo, Libra, Scorpio, Sagittarius, Capricorn, Aquarius, and Pises — it made sense to me (even without awareness of Dr. Schwartz and his work) that Ophiuchus would play the role of higher Self in the myths of the world, which have as one of their central themes the *dramatization* of our disconnection from Self, and the *way back* to reconnection with Self.

It also made sense to me that Ophiuchus would be the constellation used to represent Self by the ancient system of celestial myth found in cultures around the world because, in addition to being "hidden" or "forgotten" or "excluded," Ophiuchus is also situated "above" the twelve zodiac constellations (hence a perfect representative to play the role of "higher" Self), if we use north as "up" (and as the constellations are oriented for observers in the northern hemisphere). Further, Ophiuchus is not only situated above the twelve zodiac constellations but also, as we have just seen, Ophiuchus is situated alongside the rising path of the Milky Way galaxy, which forms a "vertical ring" in the dome of the heavens running almost perpendicular to the more "horizontal" band of the zodiac and ecliptic, a vertical ring (which we are inside) which runs up almost to the north celestial pole and which runs down almost to the south celestial pole in the heavens. Thus, Ophiuchus stands alongside the "upward path" of the Milky Way which leads in a different way from the plane of the ecliptic (the plane of our mortal existence) and represents in myth a spiritual path: the path of reconnection with Self but also the path of reconnection with the divine, and with the Invisible Realm.

I had already noticed as early as the publication of *Star Myths of the World, Volume Two: Greek Mythology* (2016) that the voyage of Odysseus described in the ancient epic of the Odyssey follows along the zodiac band, particularly the "lower" half of the zodiac band, when hours of daylight in the northern hemisphere are shorter than hours of darkness, commencing at the September equinox and proceeding "down" to the December solstice and onwards to the point of March equinox. Odysseus and his unfortunate followers would consistently make it almost to the point of March equinox before being "bounced back" down to the December solstice, again and again. It is only when the direction of the action in the epic takes a new turn, "upwards" along the Milky Way, that Odysseus can get home.

Additionally, the visit of Odysseus to the underworld, which he takes at the direction of the bewitching goddess Circe who tells him he must seek out the counsel of the dead seer Tiresias, has Odysseus being told by Tiresias that he must carry an oar on his shoulder, traveling inland until he encounters a people unfamiliar with the sea. The shade of Tiresias tells Odysseus that he will only finish his journey when another traveler falls in beside Odysseus on the road and inquires about the "winnowing fan" that Odysseus is carrying on his shoulder (meaning the ship's oar). This question will be an indication that Odysseus has reached a people completely unfamiliar with the sea, because they will mistake the ship's oar for an implement for winnowing grain.

As I have explained elsewhere, the constellation which appears to be carrying either a large oar or a winnowing fan over its shoulder is almost certainly the constellation Orion, as shown in the illustration below which juxtaposes Orion with a photograph of a woman winnowing grain using an actual winnowing fan:

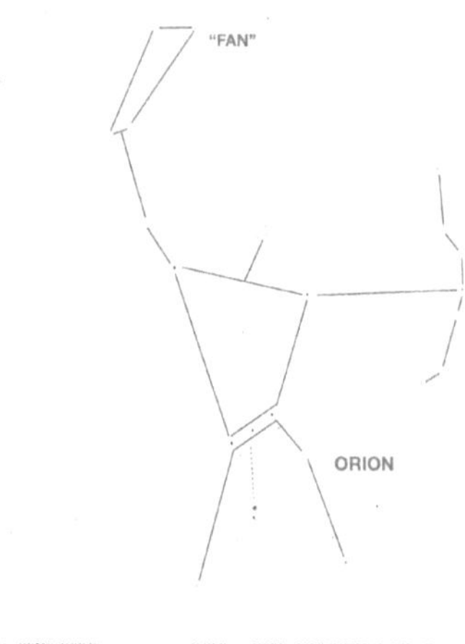

This important instruction from Tiresias can also be seen as an indication that Odysseus must travel "upwards" along the Milky Way, because the Milky Way winds past Orion as it passes through the region of the zodiac constellations Cancer and Gemini (the so-called "Gate of Cancer"). Thus, to reach Orion from the region of the December solstice (when the sun's path is down around the constellations Sagittarius and Capricorn), one could travel "upwards" along the Milky Way, past Ophiuchus and Hercules and the twin birds of Aquila and Cygnus and onwards past Pegasus and the Great Square, eventually coming to the region of Orion (of course, a reference by John the Baptist to one who would come after him, one "whose fan is in his hand," in the gospels of the Bible also refers to this constellation, as I have explained elsewhere).

Thus, the way which Odysseus must take in order to return home, and which he must eventually continue until he reaches the place where he can be reconciled with the god Poseidon, leads past Ophiuchus (and in this case continues all the way to Orion). All this to say that to an understanding of the significance of the path "upwards" along the Milky Way, besides which path the constellation Ophiuchus stands, provides still further insight into the use by the ancient myths of the constellation Ophiuchus embody higher Self in their system of celestial metaphor.

But with the expanded perspective and insight into our inner landscape afforded us by the paradigm of Dr. Richard Schwartz and Internal Family Systems, the use of Ophiuchus as the figure of Self in the ancient myths becomes all the more profound. Ophiuchus is *among* the other constellations of the zodiac, but is separate and different from them — just as Dr. Schwartz has found that Self is among all the other "parts" within our internal family, but with a completely different quality such that Self is not a "part" but rather the one who can understand our parts, who can heal our parts, and who can bring our parts into harmony.

The transformative realization that we are all *multiple* helps us to see that the various zodiac constellations through which the sun will travel in its annual cycle (and the mythical figures corresponding to those zodiac constellations in the myths, whether those figures are gods and goddesses or whether, like the brothers of Joseph in the Genesis story, they are mythical human figures) correspond to our various "parts" in the system of Dr. Schwartz. As we have already discussed, the different gods and goddesses each have gifts and resources to impart to men and women, while also possessing what we might call a "shadow side" which manifests as more unwelcome aspects of their positive traits and characteristics — and Dr. Schwartz has described our various parts in very similar terms. But Self is different from the parts, in many respects, including the fact that unlike them Self does not become polarized but instead knows instinctively how to heal the parts and to restore them from their polarization.

Self-figures in myths around the world can be shown to correspond very often to Ophiuchus, as I have explored at some length in *Myth and Trau-*

ma (particularly in chapters Seven through Ten). The figure of Joseph among his brethren, as we have just seen, dramatizes very accurately the internal paradigm described by Dr. Schwartz in IFS of the Self among the various parts, but so too does Jesus among the twelve disciples in the various gospel accounts (including not only the canonical gospels which were included in what we today call the New Testament, but also the many other gospel texts which were excluded by the founders of literalist Christianity but which were abundant during the first centuries of the "Common Era," some of which have survived in the Nag Hammadi library and other texts). Jesus clearly exhibits the inherent qualities of Self such as compassion and clarity and confidence and the rest. Like Self, Jesus can heal the most grievous of afflictions among the parts, and the Jesus story dramatizes very graphically the truth that Dr. Schwartz has observed regarding Self, that "Self is indestructible."

In fact, many myths around the world illustrate the indestructible, un-damageable nature of our deeper Self by dramatizing horrific wounds being inflicted upon figures representative of Self, not just in the Jesus story but also for example in the story of Osiris who is slain and cut into fourteen pieces and buried in a casket around which a tree later grows, but from which predicament Osiris eventually is restored. As I have shown in the chapters dealing with the myths of Egypt in *The Ancient World-Wide System*, Osiris is often identified with the constellation Orion, but there are abundant indications that he is also associated with the constellation Ophiuchus.

Similarly, the goddess Inanna in the texts of ancient Sumer is described as going down into the underworld and experiencing a series of successive humiliations, culminating in her being hung up on a hook like a side of meat for three days (in a pattern very familiar to those familiar with the story of the Crucifixion of Christ in the gospels). Despite these horrific abuses, Inanna also returns triumphantly — and, like both Jesus and Osiris, Inanna can be confidently identified with the constellation Ophiuchus as well.

Below is another illustration of the outline of Ophiuchus, showing how the constellation very naturally suggests the shape of the traditional Cross of the Crucifix in the gospel stories of Jesus — in fact, the "tripartite" nature of Ophiuchus with central body flanked by the two "serpent-halves" indicates the description in some of the gospel accounts that Jesus was crucified in between two thieves:

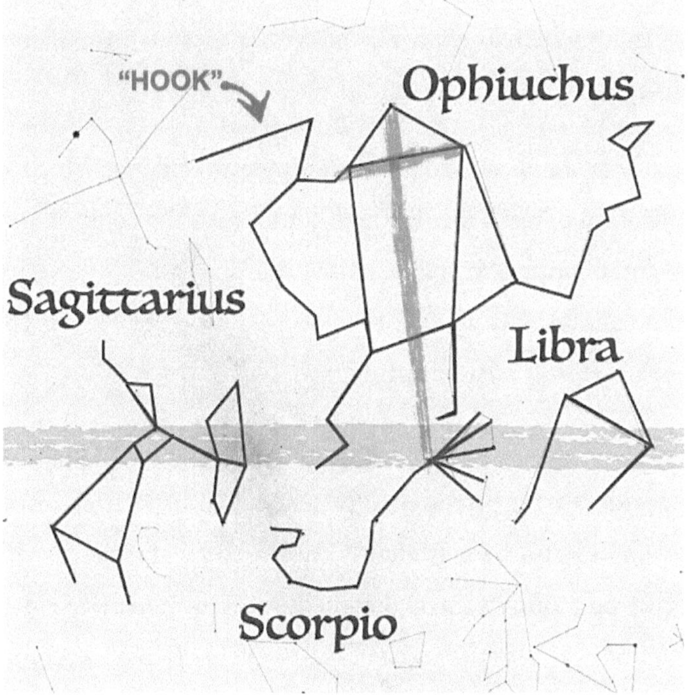

Examination of the outline of Ophiuchus will also show the heavenly inspiration for the "hook" upon which Inanna is hanged during her sojourn to the underworld, in her myth which parallels the story of Christ being hung up on a Cross and then spending three days in the grave. The "tail"-side of the flanking serpent-halves of Ophiuchus can clearly be seen to suggest the shape of a large "hook," as indicated in the star-chart above.

Additionally, as I discuss in *The Ancient World-Wide System*, the two serpent-halves on either side of the coffin-shaped central body of Ophiuchus can be seen to correspond to the "linen wrappings" that are wrapped around the chest containing the body of Osiris in the description of the Osiris and Isis story preserved in the account of Plutarch.[51] This correspondence can be seen in the star-chart above as well, although I did not label the two serpent halves as the linen winding-sheet of Osiris (and, as discussed in *Ancient World-Wide System*, there are many other details of the Osiris myth which argue for a connection between the slain god and Ophiuchus).

Myth and Trauma also discusses the abundant evidence which supports an identification of the figure of the Buddha with the constellation Ophiuchus — and of course the figure of the Buddha can also be seen to manifest all the desirable characteristics of Self described by Richard Schwartz in his Internal Family Systems paradigm.

The goddess Athena, goddess of wisdom in the myths of ancient Greece and the goddess who provides Odysseus with inspiration throughout the Odyssey, can also be confidently shown to be associated with Ophiuchus. Self is our conduit through which we connect to divine inspiration, through whom we hear the voice of the gods. In virtually every myth system we can look at, there will be a figure who dramatizes the characteristics of Self and who is often associated with the constellation Ophiuchus. In the Sanskrit texts of ancient India, there are multiple such figures, including in different stories the gods Shiva, Vishnu, and Krishna (who himself is an avatar of Vishnu) — all of whom I have previously demonstrated (for example in *Ancient World-Wide System*) to be associated with the constellation Ophiuchus.

And in Norse myth, the god Odin is the god most associated with wisdom, and he can be conclusively shown to be associated with Ophiuchus as well — although Odin is a somewhat conflicted figure for dramatizing higher Self, in that Odin is often portrayed in the myths as being divided against himself, such as in the incident of the building of the walls of Asgard, or the incident of the binding of Fenrir the Wolf. The "imperfection" of the portrayal of Self by the figure of Odin in the Norse myths can perhaps be explained by the fact that Odin is associated with other Ophiuchus-figures such as Baldr (whose connection with Ophiuchus is explored in my 2018 book *Star Myths of the World, Volume Four: Norse Mythology*), as well as the jotuns generally (whom Odin often visits, in disguise, during his quests for more wisdom) and Mimir in particular, all of whom can be seen beyond doubt to be associated with Ophiuchus, with the towering jotuns (ice-giants) being portrayed as the repositories of the most ancient wisdom in the Norse world.

One jotun whom Odin visits is named Vafthruthnir, which means "mighty weaver," a name which identifies him beyond doubt with the constellation Ophiuchus, a constellation in the heavens which frequently appears as a loom, due to its shape — and note the multiple references in the Bible to giants whose spears are invariably described as being as large as a "weaver's beam."

All of these aspects of Self, including the repeated portrayal by Ophiuchus of mythical figures who dramatize characteristics of Self, as well as evidence which supports the conclusion that it is through Self that we receive insight and inspiration that appears to go beyond anything explainable with conventional materialist paradigms, have been discussed at some length in *Myth and Trauma*. But by adding the understanding of Self's role in harmonizing the multiple parts in our Internal Family System provided by Dr. Schwartz, we can glean additional insights into what the ancient myths are trying to show us.

First, as already touched upon thus far in the book, Self figures in myth can harmonize and reconcile the often-contentious figures representing our *internal family* in those same myths. In the story of Joseph, for example, the multiple brothers plot to do away with their brother Joseph, and end up "burying" him in a pit before selling him to a passing caravan. But Joseph later exhibits compassion and love for these brothers and effects a reconciliation between them. And in the Greek myths, as we have already noted, the twelve Olympian gods (which, like the children of Jacob or Israel in the Bible, also number more than twelve) are also all related as part of one big and sometimes contentious family.

Gods of other myths are also often members of one large family. Such is the case with the deities of ancient Mesopotamia, including the related pantheons of the Sumerians and later Babylonians, as well as with the various pantheons of ancient Egypt. Such can also be seen to be the case with the gods and goddesses of ancient Japan whose genealogy is recited in the KoJiKi, or Record of Ancient Matters. And we can continue around the globe, finding similar examples in the myths of other cultures. In the Maui myths of the Polynesian cultures of the Pacific, Maui himself is one of several brothers who, similar to the brothers of Joseph, resent their youngest brother — but who are all, interestingly enough, named Maui as well! From this detail we could perhaps surmise that all the "multiple Mauis" not only represent one internal family but that the myths are giving us an extra nod towards seeing that this internal family represents the internal landscape of *one individual*.

Giorgio de Santillana and Hertha von Dechend, the authors of *Hamlet's Mill: an essay on myth and the frame of time*, a seminal work which demonstrates the existence of a world-wide system operating in ancient myth and ritual and folklore from cultures separated by vast distances and across millennia, document the recurring pattern of the god who comes down to dwell among men and women, ruling over a long-lost "Golden Age," but who at some point departs, traveling away across the ocean, or in some cases going down to sleep beneath the waves. Another recurring aspect of this pattern is that the benevolent divine figure promises to one day return, bringing back that Golden Age and restoring harmony.

The book's title comes from the great mill-stone of the heavens, which has become unhinged, knocked off-kilter, and is now grinding out pain and suffering instead of peace and plenty. The authors point out that in early versions of the Northern European myths of a figure named Amlodhi, which furnished the pattern for the figure of Hamlet in the play of Shakespeare, Amlodhi has a great mill-stone which is knocked into the sea.

In the story of *Hamlet*, of course, young Hamlet is filled with doubt over the right course of action after he begins to suspect that his father, the rightful king, has been killed by his father's wicked brother, Hamlet's uncle. As the authors of *Hamlet's Mill* point out, this pattern is an ancient one, and can be found in the myths of Osiris in ancient Egypt, in which the rightful king Osiris is slain by his scheming brother Set, later to be avenged by the son of Osiris and Isis. In modern film, we see the very same pattern play out in the plot of the movie *The Lion King* (1994).

The murder of Osiris, who is then placed into a coffin and cast into the sea, follows the pattern described in *Hamlet's Mill* of the benevolent god who rules over a Golden Age but who goes away to sleep beyond the sea (or, in some cases, beneath the waves), but who will one day return. De Santillana and von Dechend write:

> That things are not as they used to be, that the world is obviously going from bad to worse, seems to have been an established idea throughout the ages. The unhinging of the Mill is caused by the shifting of the world axis. [. . .] It churned once gold, then salt, and today sand and stones. [. . .] But right now, there is at least one age designated as the first, when the Mill ground out peace and plenty. It is the Golden Age, in Latin tradition, *Saturnia regna*, the reign of Saturn; in Greek, Kronos. In this dim perplexing figure there is an extraordinary concordance throughout world myths. In India it was Yama, in the Old Persian *Avesta* it was Yima xsaēta, a name which became in New Persian Jamshyd; in Latin Saeturnus, then Saturnus. Saturn or Kronos in many names had been known as the Ruler of the Golden Age, of that time when men knew not war and bloody sacrifices, not the inequality of classes — Lord of Justice and Measures, as Enki since Sumerian days, the Yellow Emperor and legislator in China.[52]

So, Saturn-figures in myth around the world are associated with a preceding (but now lost, and only dimly-remembered) Golden Age, during which peace and prosperity reigned, and there was neither war nor class inequality. And, the authors of *Hamlet's Mill* point out (following the ancient texts as well as preceding mythical analysis by other scholars) another crucially-important aspect of these Saturnian figures world-wide is the understanding that they *came down to this earth* and *dwelt among men and women* during that long-ago Golden Age.

De Santillana and von Dechend write:

> A ruler who "means well" is a Saturnian figure. No one but Saturn dwelt among men. Says an Orphic fragment: "Orpheus reminds us that Saturn dwelt openly on earth and among men." Dionysius of Halicarnassus (I.36.1) writes: "Thus before the reign of Zeus, Kronos ruled on this very earth," to which Maximilian Mayer crisply annotates: "We find no mention anywhere of such an earthly sojourn on the part of Zeus."53

Why is it that these "Saturnian figures" are distinctly noted in ancient myth for this particular trait of coming down to earth to dwell among us?

The authors of *Hamlet's Mill*, who deserve enormous credit for perceiving the very existence and the outlines of the lost ancient system uniting mythology across all the inhabited continents and islands of our planet, nevertheless did not quite grasp the critical connection between the characters of those myths and the *specific constellations* in our night sky which form the most important backbone of that system. In this case of Saturnian figures, they do not perceive that Saturn himself, as well as his parallels in other myths around the globe, corresponds to the constellation

Ophiuchus — and that this connection opens up absolutely invaluable new perspectives for our deeper understanding!

We can see from several details in the ancient texts that Saturn (and his counterpart Kronos of ancient Greece), with his great sickle or scythe, corresponds to the figure of Ophiuchus in the heavens, grasping what we have already identified as the "hook-shaped" tail of the serpent (on the east side of the constellation's central body):

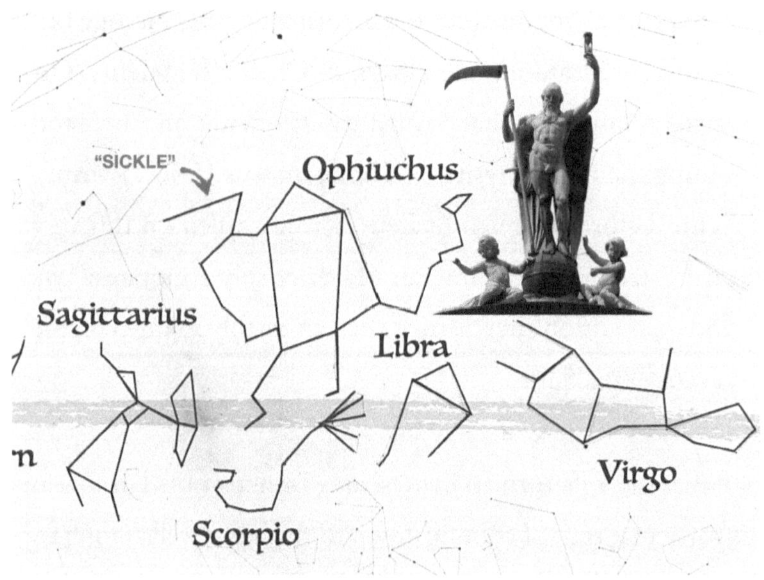

In the image above, which superimposes an admittedly modern statue of Saturn found atop the building of the Naturmuseum Senckenberg in Frankfurt, we can see the resemblance of the "tail-side" of the two serpent-halves flanking the central body of the constellation Ophiuchus to the great sickle or scythe carried by Saturn or Kronos, which is described in ancient texts as early as that of the Theogony of Hesiod.

In the Theogony, we read of the bringing forth of this sickle by Gaia as a weapon against Ouranos in her anger against the imprisonment of the Cyclopes and other gigantic offspring of Gaia and Ouranos. Of her children, only Kronos had the courage to take the sickle and raise up his hand against his father Ouranos. The Theogony tells us:

> Then his son reached out from ambush with his left hand, and with his right he grasped the monstrous sickle, long and jagged-toothed, and eagerly he reaped the genitals from his dear father and threw them behind him to be borne away. [. . .] And when at first he had cut off the genitals with the adamant and thrown them into the sea, they were borne along the water for a long time, and a white foam rose up around them from the immortal flesh, and inside this grew a maiden. First she approached holy Cythera, and from there she went on to sea-girt Cyprus. She came forth, a reverend, beautiful goddess, and grass grew up around her beneath her slender feet. Gods and men call her "Aphrodite," the foam-born goddess, and also "Cytherea" since she arrived at Cythera [. . .].[54]

As we can see, the ancient text itself specifies that Kronos held the long sickle in his right hand — and that in the preceding image shown above, the statue of Saturn also shows the god holding the sickle in the right hand. Admittedly this is a modern-era depiction, but it corresponds to the ancient text — and also to the outline of the actual constellation Ophiuchus in the sky! We can clearly see from the star-chart itself that Ophiuchus is holding the "sickle" on the *left* side of the central body as we face the constellation, which would of course be the *right* hand of a person (assuming that we envision the figure associated with Ophiuchus as facing towards us rather than turning his or her back to us).

In the modern statue, Saturn holds an upraised hourglass in the opposite hand (the hand on the right side of the statue as we face it and it faces us, which is the left hand). The constellation Ophiuchus, of course, has the "serpent's head" on this side, which previous books have shown can be envisioned in different myths as a wine goblet, a small mirror, a lotus flower, a piece of fruit, a gouged-out eyeball, and any number of other items which it can be seen to resemble. Note the similarity in the actual outline of stars to a wine-glass, and in doing so we can see how the similarity to an hour-glass could be extrapolated. Kronos and Saturn are associated with measuring out time, although Hesiod's poem nowhere mentions an hour-glass, so we will pass over that detail and continue on to one other interesting aspect of the modern statue shown in the image above: the fact that the Saturn figure is depicted as standing upon an Earth-globe with a line running across it like a belt, evocative of the Earth's equator.

As we can see from the star-chart and as we have already examined at length, the constellation Ophiuchus stands with one foot just within the line created by the plane of the ecliptic, the ecliptic being the path of the sun's travel through the year and the defining line which passes through the zodiac. As I have explained at some length in my on-demand online course entitled *Celestial Mechanics and the Myths*, the authors of *Hamlet's Mill* present solid evidence and analysis which argues that the ancient esoteric system underlying the myths envisions the plane of the ecliptic as "the world" or "this Earthly plane." As evidence, they cite strong evidence from the myths of many different cultures which shows beyond debate that when the ages-long motion of precession eventually "delays" the background of stars enough to cause the sun's rising point on the March equinox, June solstice, September equinox, and December solstice to shift into a whole different set of four zodiac constellations, this momentous change would be encoded in the ancient texts and sacred stories as "the end of the world" or the creation of a "new Earth."

The authors of *Hamlet's Mill* write:

> First, what was the "earth"? In the most general sense, the "earth" was the ideal plane laid through the ecliptic [. . .] "earth" is the ideal plane going through the four points of the year, the equinoxes and the solstices. Since the four constellations rising heliacally at the two equinoxes and the two solstices determine and define an "earth," it is termed quadrangular [. . .]. And since constellations rule the four corners of the quadrangular earth only temporarily, such an "earth" can rightly be said to perish, and a new earth to rise from the waters, with four new constellations rising at the four points of the year.[55]

Based on this understanding, we can see why, as the ancient writer Dionysius of Halicarnassus (born around 50 BC) says of Kronos in a pattern which will hold true for other Saturnian figures that "before the reign of Zeus, Kronos reigned on this very earth." Saturnian figures are characterized by dwelling on Earth among men and women because Ophiuchus stands within the circle of the zodiac defined by the ecliptic.

Figures associated with Ophiuchus who dwell among us and yet are divine include of course Jesus of the gospels, who as already mentioned can be shown beyond doubt to be associated with Ophiuchus. Jesus also exhibits the characteristics described in *Hamlet's Mill* of eventually going away and leaving his followers with the promise that one day he will return.

In the case of Saturn, who ruled over the Golden Age but then went away to sleep beneath the waves, we find one description of this ancient myth in a text by Plutarch entitled "Concerning the Face which Appears in the Orb of the Moon." In that text, Plutarch explains that when Jupiter overthrew his father Saturn (as in the Greek myth Zeus overthrew his father Kronos), Jupiter imprisoned Saturn upon the island of Ogygia, lying in the arms of Ocean. There, Plutarch relates, it is said that Saturn lies asleep "in the deep cave of a hollow rock, shining like fine gold, Jupiter having prepared sleep instead of fetters and shackles to keep him from stirring."[56]

We can see the very same pattern of the benevolent king who, having presided over a Golden Age, goes down to sleep beneath the waters in the story of King Arthur in the Arthurian legends, as the authors of *Hamlet's Mill* point out.[57] De Santillana and von Dechend note that "The mere notion of the emperors sleeping makes it clear that they are expected to awake and to return one day."[58] In addition to the sleeping King Arthur and "Ogygian Kronos himself," the authors of *Hamlet's Mill* also add to this list the god Quetzalcoatl of the Aztecs, whose land is in the central region of modern Mexico.

Graham Hancock explores the profusion of this myth-pattern throughout the Americas in his 1995 book *Fingerprints of the Gods*. Examining the sixteenth- and seventeenth-century accounts recorded by Spanish conquistadors, including the Roman Catholic clergy who sought to denounce and destroy the received ancient wisdom of the inhabitants of the lands of Central and South America encountered during the invasion, Graham finds that across the Inca, Maya and Aztec cultures there were very strong traditions relating the arrival in previous days of a tall, authoritative, benevolent civilizing figure who taught the people to be good to one another and not to fight, but instead to show charity to each and every individual, and who was called by the Andean cultures Ticci Viracocha.[59]

Graham goes on to explain: "Other names applied to the same figure included Huaracocha, Con, Con Ticci or Kon Tiki, Thunapa, Taapac, Tupaca and Illa."[60] As he shows, all these different figures across multiple ancient cultures of the Americas share the same characteristics, characteristics that the authors of *Hamlet's Mill* would identify as part of the world-wide Saturnian pattern: a civilizing figure, who teaches humanity to love one another and treat one another with kindness and respect, visiting during a past age but eventually leaving with the promise to one day return. In some instances of this pattern, this benevolent figure will be described as going down beneath the waves to sleep until his return, as with Saturn in Ogygia or Arthur in the lake of Avalon, but in other cases he will go away across the sea, and this is the aspect of the pattern most prevalent in the traditions of Central and South America recorded by the early Spanish invaders and examined by Graham Hancock in *Fingerprints of the Gods*.

The accounts consistently describe this benevolent figure, one of whose names is Viracocha, as a carrying a staff and dressing in a cloak which reached far down his legs — characteristics consistent with the outline of Ophiuchus itself and of figures in myth around the world who can be confidently identified with Ophiuchus. And, as Graham Hancock points out, the name Viracocha means "foam of the sea," just as the name Aphrodite in Greek also refers to the foam of the sea.[61] This connection can be explained by the fact that the constellation Ophiuchus itself stands with one foot in the Milky Way, which is why Viracocha as a figure associated with Ophiuchus receives this name, and why he is always described as departing over the water when he makes his poignant good-bye.

This association is further strengthened by the fact that the accounts of the South American cultures describe Viracocha as disappearing into the west (in some accounts he made his way to the region of modern-day Ecuador before he stepped into the sea, promising to return, while in others he disappears across Lake Titicaca but eventually makes his way from there down to the sea). In both cases, this would mean that his point of departure was from the west coast of South America, into the Pacific, and thus that his direction was into the west.

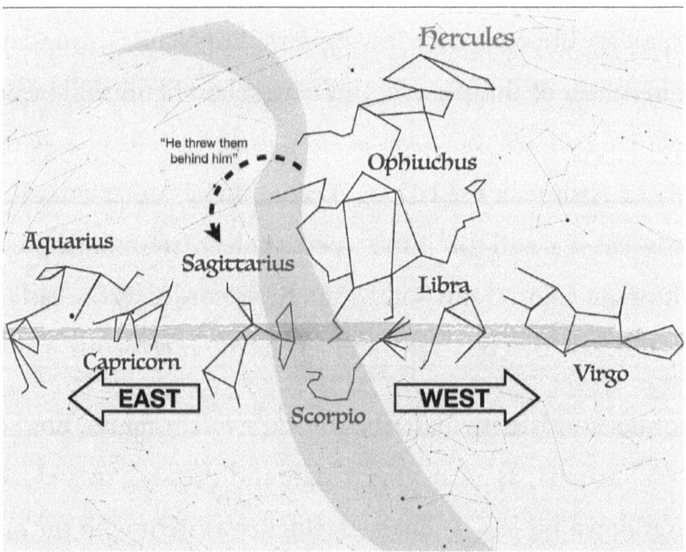

Similarly, in the Greek myth of the generation of Aphrodite, as we saw in the passage from Hesiod's Theogony cited earlier, it was an Ophiuchus figure (Kronos) who dared to grasp the great sickle and castrate his father Ouranos — and who then threw the genitals "behind him" to be borne away by the sea. I have previously argued, for example in *Star Myths of the World, Volume Two*, that the goddess Aphrodite is likely associated with the constellation Sagittarius, a constellation which plays the role of a beautiful woman or a beautiful goddess in many myths. Thus, if Ophiuchus plays the role of sickle-wielding Kronos, and if Kronos throws the members of Ouranos "behind him" after castrating his father, then it appears that in some myths Ophiuchus is envisioned as moving towards the west (because this would mean that Sagittarius is "behind" Ophiuchus). Thus, after throwing the genitals into the sea, Aphrodite arises out of the sea-foam (the Milky Way), thus explaining why the male figure of Viracocha (who disappears over the sea-foam into the west) and the female figure of Aphrodite (who is generated from the sea-foam "behind" Ophiuchus) both have names which signify "the foam of the sea."

As an additional important aside, note that in the star-chart above I have included the outline of the constellation Hercules, directly above Ophiuchus. In myth, figures associated with Ophiuchus are often "descended from" figures associated with Hercules, because Ophiuchus can be seen to be directly below Hercules and hence "descended" from that constellation. If this is the case, then Ouranos the father of Kronos, whom Kronos castrates with the great sickle, would be associated with the constellation Hercules — and we can see from the position of the two constellations in the sky why the constellations became the foundation for such a violent mythological episode. The figure of Hercules, as we have already discussed in some detail, is notable for its very deep lunging posture, with legs far apart — and the long, jagged sickle of Ophiuchus is held in such a way that a figure associated with Ophiuchus such as Kronos could be imagined to be threatening castration to the figure just above.

From all these pieces of evidence, we can confidently conclude that Viracocha and his other parallels in the ancient traditions and sacred stories of the people of the Americas matches the pattern of a god or god-like figure who comes down to Earth to dwell among men and women, teaching peace and beneficial skills, instituting a Golden Age of harmony and plenty, and then disappearing into water with a promise of return — and, significantly and strikingly, we see that all these "Saturnian" figures are associated beyond any doubt with the constellation Ophiuchus, the so-called "thirteenth zodiac sign," which dwells among them but is not one of them, a hidden sign and an excluded sign but one who is "above" the others and which we have seen to represent higher Self in the myths of the world (including the stories of the Bible).

What are these stories dramatizing for us about the nature of Self? They show us that Self is god-like in nature — and in fact, Self is *our connection* with the divine. Jesus, who is definitely associated with the constellation Ophiuchus, famously says in the gospel of John: "I am the way, the truth, and the life: no man cometh unto the Father, but by me" (John 14: 6).

Note from the previous diagram showing the relative locations of Hercules and Ophiuchus that, if the Father of Jesus is associated with Hercules (as the God of the Bible is undoubtedly proven to be, and as I demonstrate repeatedly in other books and in my online courses of the *Celestial Bible Tour* series), which makes sense in the logic of the world-wide myth system in which figures associated with Ophiuchus are often "descended from" figures associated with Hercules, that Ophiuchus is indeed "the way" (that is, the road or the path) to the Father (that is, the constellation Hercules), and thus the *intermediary* between the "Earth" of the zodiac and the divine. It is *through* higher Self that we have contact with the divine, and receive inspiration from the Invisible Realm.

Self is calm, confident, and knows just what to do in all situations — and these characteristics are dramatized in the figures of Viracocha, or Jesus, or the Buddha, or the other "Golden Age" rulers. But in these stories, the figure who portrays these benevolent and desirable characteristics of Self goes away, sometimes to be buried or entombed beneath the waves: what aspect of our authentic Self does this pattern reveal?

Clearly, it demonstrates for us the same truth that is demonstrated by the story of Joseph being thrown down into a pit by his brothers: the fact that, through trauma and what some psychologists including Dr. Richard Schwartz refer to as "attachment injury," we can lose connection with Self, we can bury or even banish our authentic, deep, and, in fact, *divine* Self. But — as with the stories of Viracocha, and Saturn, and Jesus, and King Arthur — there is a promised return in the old stories dramatizing Self and our loss of Self (or rather, loss of *connection* with Self). We have the promise of reconnection — because Self is never really gone, and Self cannot be killed or destroyed, no matter what happens in our lives and no matter what trauma we experience.

Clearly, we need Self to live our "best life" (just as Saturnian Self-figures in the myths rule over a "Golden Age") — but how? How do we recover that connection with Self, and restore that harmony among all the different parts and personalities of our internal family?

One answer that comes back to us from the myths to the question of "how" is simple: just ask!

In the story of Solomon found in the text of 1 Kings, we are told that near the beginning of his reign, Solomon went to the great high place of Gibeon, in order to offer burnt offerings there. A "great high place" itself is associated with Ophiuchus, and I have demonstrated in my book examining the Norse myths that the Lidskjalf (also spelled Hlidskjalf) or "high seat" of the wisdom-god Odin can be conclusively shown to be associated with the constellation of Ophiuchus, as can Odin himself. There, in the great high place, the ancient text of the books of Kings in the Bible tell us: "In Gibeon the LORD appeared to Solomon in a dream by night: and God said, Ask what I shall give thee" (1 Kings 3: 5).

We can see this episode as a clear parallel to the Judgement of Paris we explored in the previous chapter. In that myth from ancient Greece, the gods offered Paris wisdom, fame in battle, rulership over kingdoms — but Paris chose instead to have as his wife the most beautiful woman in the world, leading to disaster and destruction. Similarly, in the parallel story of King Midas, who was presented by the god Dionysus with a similar offer to ask for anything, Midas in his greed for even more wealth than he already possessed asked for the golden touch, with similarly disastrous results.

In the case of Solomon, however, the young king asks for wisdom — and is granted "a wise and an understanding heart," (1 Kings 3: 11), such that there was never any before or since with such wisdom. Solomon, of course, is yet another Ophiuchus figure, and (as I have demonstrated in *Star Myths of the Bible*) when God gives him a wise and an understanding heart, we can see this portrayed in the heavens by the figure of Hercules reaching down to "give" Ophiuchus the heart-shape seen at the "serpent head" side of that constellation.

The implication from all of these various myths is that *divine wisdom is available to us for the asking*.

In fact, we already have access to the divine, and the clarity and courage and confidence and creativity associated with divine inspiration, right now, within us. We all, no matter our background and no matter what kind of trauma, or attachment injury, or heartbreak we have experienced, have this indestructible Self — although our parts in an act of automatic and unconscious self-defense may have pushed that Self down to "sleep beneath the waves."

We just have to learn how to allow this deep Self to rise again — and the myths demonstrate over and over that Self will return. But first, we need to actually understand that Self exists, which is a big step for many of us because the suppression of Self takes place as a result of trauma and heartbreak, heartbreak so painful that the parts of our internal family who pushed Self down into that pit don't even want to admit that it happened, because they are trying to block that trauma out and avoid having to ever feel it again.

But, as we saw with the example of the conversation between Dr. Schwartz and his anorexic client Margie, Self can emerge spontaneously, when we ask other parts to step aside or step back. These parts take on roles in an effort to defend the internal family and to suppress deep hurts and heartbreaks and feelings of shame or insecurity or worthlessness. In doing so, Dr. Schwartz explains, they can "eclipse" or overshadow Self, such that those desirable qualities of Self are replaced with (or "blended with" as he calls it) the qualities of the part.[62]

In *No Bad Parts*, Dr. Schwartz explains:

> It's important to remember that regardless of how blended we are, the Self is still in there — it never goes away. In ancient times, when there was a solar eclipse and it suddenly got dark because the moon blocked the sun, people would panic, believing the sun had disappeared. Like the sun, the Self can be temporarily obscured, but it never disappears.

When the moon passes by or the clouds dissipate, the sun shines as brightly as ever. Similarly, when parts unblend, the Self's nourishing energy is readily available again and the parts are comforted to sense the presence of such a strong, loving inner leader.[63]

In upcoming chapters we will explore further what the myths have to say about allowing Self to shine forth. But before ending this chapter, there are a few practical applications we can consider based upon some of the ancient stories we have seen so far.

First, we can notice the importance of dreams. In the story of Joseph which opened this chapter, we can see that Joseph exhibits clarity about the ways to prepare Egypt for the upcoming years of famine, thus saving many lives including those of his brothers and parents, as well as displaying compassion and love for his brothers even after they had long ago thrown him down into a pit and then sent him down to bondage and servitude in Egypt.

One of Joseph's distinguishing features in the stories is his ability to interpret dreams. Dreams can be a source of inspiration and messages which seem to originate in a realm beyond what we experience as ordinary reality. In this chapter I have argued that Self is our connection to that realm described variously in the different ancient myth-systems around the world as the divine realm or the Invisible Realm — or even, in the wisdom preserved by the Indigenous Aboriginal cultures of Australia, as the Dreamtime.

It is through Self that we experience connection with this realm, and it is through Self that we can interpret what meaning such inspiration may have for us.

When we sleep, those protectors in our conscious mind relax their guard, which can allow our deep Self to arise. However, the ancient myths also warn us that not everything that we perceive in dreams can be accepted uncritically as an inspiration from the divine — discernment is necessary, which is why they require Self to be interpreted, as opposed to parts (and it is likely that parts can also speak to us in dreams, as they process the various events that dot our internal landscape, even though our conscious mind is not in control once we go to sleep).

In the Odyssey, there is an important passage in which Penelope, the long-suffering wife of the missing hero Odysseus, expresses the ancient understanding that dreams must be examined carefully in order to determine whether their message is true or false. In Book 19 of the Odyssey, Penelope is entertaining unawares her long-lost husband Odysseus, who has returned but disguised as an old beggar, clothed in rags. Penelope confides to her guest that she has had a dream in which an eagle swoops down and kills all her geese, and then settles on a rafter and addresses her with a human voice, telling her that he is in fact her husband, returned to her at last, and that the geese were her suitors, who had been lounging about her house and devouring all its wealth.

Odysseus in disguise tells her that such a dream can only mean one thing: Odysseus shall return and bring destruction upon each and every one of those unwelcome suitors. But Penelope objects by telling him that there are two gates through which dreams come to us, one gate made of carved ivory, and the other of polished horn. Those dreams which come through the ivory gate, she explains, are but phantoms, while those which proceed through the gate of horn are filled with truth.[64]

Thus, the ancient sources clearly indicate that dreams are important, but that we must be discerning in their interpretation. Nevertheless, it is clear from the record of ancient myth, as well as from traditions which have survived in cultures where literalist Christianity did not eradicate the ancient wisdom until more recent centuries, that altered states of consciousness can be a gateway for reconnection with Self.

Such altered states of consciousness can of course be achieved using naturally occurring substances, including certain mushrooms, cannabis, tobacco, and others, as chronicled in Mircea Eliade's groundbreaking book *Shamanism: Archaic Techniques of Ecstasy*, first published in 1951.

However, as Eliade's research also documents, and as we have already seen in our earlier exploration of techniques such as dancing which leads to possession by an Orisha, human experience has also found numerous other paths to achieving altered states of consciousness which can lead to communication with the Invisible Realm and which may also help us to reconnect with Self. Among those described by Eliade and used by shamanic traditions in cultures around the world are rhythmic drumming, chanting, whirling, rhythmic rattling with a rattle, and the use of a variety of ascetic disciplines including what the book describes as "mystical heat" and which is used in certain Tibetan ascetic traditions involving sitting naked in a snowstorm or drying wet sheets placed on the body through the generation of internal heat.[65]

I myself have personally found that the experience of practicing Wim Hof Method breath-work and cold-work under the guidance of Wim Hof Method master instructor Brandon Powell while leading retreats in the mountains of Utah near Bryce Canyon and Zion National Parks can lead directly to the arrival of the presence of Self. In each of these two practices, the deliberate introduction of an uncomfortable situation leads to an initial rushing-in of "protector" voices who over-react but whose motive is obviously self-preservation and the survival instinct.

During the Wim Hof Method breathing practice, a series of deep breaths and complete exhalations brings the body to a more oxygen-infused and higher-alkaline state, followed by a "breath-hold" after a complete exhale, during which you don't take a breath inward but instead hold your breath on empty lungs instead of the usual way that we hold our breath with lungs completely full. As Wim Hof explains, "Holding your breath here will be fairly easy because your newfound alkalinity lessens the body's need for oxygen. You may be surprised to learn that you can easily hold your breath and go without any air in your lungs for thirty seconds, a minute, even a minute and a half at this point."[66]

However, even though the body does not need oxygen and there is no immediate danger of suffocation (after all, you can always just take a new inhaled breath at any moment that you feel you absolutely must), I have found that panicky protector parts speak up right away during these breath-holds, especially the first time I ever practiced this Wim Hof Method breath-work. "You need to breathe: now!" they say, or they might say: "Well, you made it through the last breath-hold, but you can't make it through this one!"

The remarkable and revealing thing that happens during these breath-holds, however, is that after those initial panicking voices of the protectors subsides (or if you calmly thank them for their concern and ask them if they will just step aside for a bit while you practice the discipline), a different presence will emerge, calmly informing your entire internal team: "We got this. I've got you. I've got you."

It is the voice of Self, and it is unmistakable.

It's a very powerful experience, and one that anyone can practice everyday. Wim Hof has outlined the method on his website and even provides short videos which anyone can play, free of charge, to hear him guide the inhales and exhales and the breath-holds.

I have found that the Wim Hof Method cold-work produces very much the same experience of initial shock accompanied by panicked, startled protectors who complain that "We need to get out now!" But when we focus on the breath and allow those protective voices to calm down (or confidently reassure them, thanking them for their concern, and asking them to trust for a moment and step back), the same unmistakable presence of our deeper Self will arise, holding the internal family and assuring them: "It's okay — I have you; I am right here; we got this."

We can experience a very similar pattern without having to plunge into a pool of icy water by simply turning the hot water off at the tap at the end of a warm shower, and standing in a cold-water shower for thirty seconds, sixty seconds, or as long as two or three minutes (the ice-bath shown above, in the snows of Duck Creek Village, Utah during the 2023 Contact at the Canyons event, lasted for three minutes of full-body immersion). This practice is also detailed in the Wim Hof Method, and can become a daily routine which brings Self to the fore.

There are many ways that we can foster the presence of Self, and we will explore this subject in greater detail as we continue. But as we conclude, recall that at the very beginning of the chapter, we saw in the opening scenes of the Iliad that the plague sent by Apollo was not stopped until the initial cause of the god's anger was identified, and the god appeased. From this and other examples throughout the ancient myths, we can see that ultimately, our recovery of Self will require that we seek to identify and then to address those deep hurts which caused us to lose contact with our Self in the first place.

Chapter Four

The forlorn exile

In the text of the gospel according to Matthew, after the Last Supper and prior to the arrest of Jesus, Jesus and his disciples sing a hymn, and then go out to the Mount of Olives (Matthew 26: 30). The very next thing the text tells us is that Jesus addresses his disciples and tells them: "All of you will be offended because of me this night" (Matthew 26: 31). Then Peter specifically declares that even if all men were to become offended because of Jesus, Peter himself would never be offended.

The word in the original Greek text which is translated "be offended" is *skandalizō*, which of course is similar to our English word "scandalized," and it means to be indignant, annoyed, or highly displeased at the actions or behavior of another. Thus Peter, being told by Jesus that they would all be scandalized or offended "because of me this night," replies: "Though all should be offended because of thee, I will never be offended" (Matthew 26: 33).

But to this declaration of loyalty, Jesus says to Peter: "Verily I say unto thee, that this night, before the cock crow, thou shalt deny me thrice" (Matthew 26: 34). Then Peter confidently rejoins, "Though I should die with thee, yet would I not deny thee," and all the other disciples after Peter, the text says, affirmed the same (Matthew 26: 35).

All the four canonical gospels recount a very similar exchange between Jesus and Peter (in Mark 14, Luke 22, and John 13). And all four texts describe a scene in which Peter sits down by a fire, while Jesus having been seized in the garden and put under arrest is being interrogated by the high priest in front of the scribes and elders, and is approached by those who recognize Peter as being one of the disciples of Jesus. The details of these encounters with those accusing Peter of being with Jesus vary so widely that it should be difficult for literalists to maintain that they all unerringly describe the same literal and historical episode, with the Mark account even describing a cock crowing once after the first denial when the other accounts only have the cock crowing after the third denial (and the other accounts having Jesus say the denials would take place before the cock would even crow at all, while only Mark's account has Jesus saying "before the cock shall crow *twice*," which seems to be a fairly significant discrepancy and hard to ignore if one wants to read the stories as strictly literal history) — but in each case, Peter vehemently denies having been ever associated with Jesus, and in most of the accounts adds that he does not even know who Jesus is!

These dramatic denials of Jesus by Peter are gut-wrenching and uncomfortable to read, made all the more so by the device of the sudden crowing of the rooster who fulfills the earlier prediction by Jesus that Peter would deny him, despite Peter's pledge that he would never do so, even if it meant Peter's life.

What happened? Peter, by all accounts the leader of the disciples, the one who was given the name of "Rock" by Jesus, the one who in fact had bravely tried to defend Jesus in the scene of his arrest in the garden, cutting off the ear of one of those who came to seize Jesus (as we learn in John 18: 26), the same Peter who vociferously protested when Jesus said that all his disciples would be offended or scandalized because of him that night, and who had said he would never deny Jesus, even at the risk of his own life, repeatedly "throws Jesus under the bus" and distances himself from him.

It is an ugly episode, a distasteful scene, and an embarrassing one. The weight of the betrayal is emphasized in one of the four texts (the Luke account) which tells us, immediately after the cock crows, "and the Lord turned, and looked upon Peter" (Luke 22: 61). In each case (excepting the John account), the text tells us that when he hears the cock crow, Peter remembers the earlier exchange with Jesus, and being filled with remorse, weeps bitterly.

How could Peter, this devoted disciple and staunch defender of Jesus in the garden, betray Jesus like that, even to the point of denying any knowledge of who he is? The text of Mark 14: 71 says of Peter during his betrayal encounter: "Then he began to curse and swear, saying, I know not this man of whom ye speak," and the other accounts dramatize similar vehement denials. What has come over him?

If this episode were a literal historical event, and Peter a literal and historical personage, we might say that the gravity of the situation, with Jesus now being in the process of being sentenced to death by crucifixion, has shocked Peter into such fear that he, fearing for his own life now, changes from defender to denier. Perhaps he was full of adrenaline when he cut off the ear of one who came to arrest Jesus, and thus did not think about the consequences, but now — seeing Jesus arrested — Peter is in a completely different frame of mind. These, or many other scenarios, could explain such a turnaround, if indeed these ancient texts were describing an actual, historical event in which Peter, trying to warm himself by the fire while keeping close enough to hear what is going on with the accusations being brought against Jesus, is approached by multiple people who saw Peter with Jesus and accused him of being one of the disciples of Jesus.

But it is not a literal and historical event, and Peter is not a literal and historical personage. The betrayal of Jesus described in these ancient texts can be shown to be celestial metaphor of the very same type as the story of Joseph thrown down into the well by his brothers, which we examined in the preceding chapter. It is a dramatization of the betrayal and denial of our own authentic Self, as a response to heartbreaking attachment injury or trauma, designed to awaken us to the fact that this suppression of Self has actually happened — because that heartbreaking trauma is so painful that we, like Peter, will then deny all knowledge of Self.

Suppression of Self caused by psychological trauma is like a crime scene in which the perpetrators have beaten and stripped the victim and shoved him into a foot locker, and when the police suddenly show up, they sit nonchalantly on the lid of the trunk, ignoring the pounding of the one they have stuffed inside.

"Self? What Self, officer? What are you talking about?" they ask innocently, even as the muffled cries of the victim can be heard from within the foot locker on which they are sitting.

But, as the doctors and healers who work in the field of trauma and who understand the psychology of the situation and the way we are pro-grammed to react, as an innate survival mechanism, the suppression and denial of Self takes place *automatically* and *without conscious decision* on our part. We suppress and deny who we are because we are wired to do so and can hardly do otherwise, although it may seem inexplicable on first glance.

In a conversation between cutting-edge healers Dr. Gabor Maté and Dr. Laurence Heller exploring the subject of how turning against and suppressing Self is actually a built-in and necessary psychological adaptation, Dr. Heller, who is a clinical therapist and developer of the NeuroAffective Relational Model for dealing with complex attachment, relational and emotional trauma, explains:

> Part of the child's adaptation to trauma is to turn against the Self. It distorts their sense of Self. [. . .] And so there's *a lot invested* in seeing the parent as good and them as bad -- because if they're bad, they can make themselves better, or at least they have this idea they can make themselves better, and win love. And they do that, unfortunately, this is part of the paradox, by giving up and disconnecting from parts of themselves [. . .].[67]

To this, Dr. Gabor Maté, whose extensive work in exploring the role of trauma and separation for Self and my view of its vital relevance to our understanding of the message of the ancient myths is discussed at some length in *Myth and Trauma*, adds:

> That's exactly what I get people to, is: OK, you're a kid, and you're three years old, and your father was yelling at your mother. Which is safer for you to believe: that your parents are bad, and they don't love you? Or that they're

incompetent, and the world isn't safe? Or is it safer for you to believe that there's something wrong with you? That you're not good enough, and that you're to be ashamed of? Obviously, it's unendurable for the child to even entertain the first hypothesis. It's much safer to turn on themselves, and then hope to change themselves, but still believe that, 'If I'm good enough, I'll be loved.'[68]

This conversation, and the wider body of work produced by these two doctors, including books written by each, can enable us to understand the mechanics of this often-misunderstood concept of "suppression of" or "disconnection from" Self. What they are describing is a coping mechanism, an adapting mechanism, indeed a *survival* mechanism, in which we are designed to "turn on ourselves," as Dr. Maté phrases it in the quotation above, in order to deal with what he calls an *unendurable* situation.

In the situation described, the child is faced with a terrifying situation, in this case a father who is yelling at the mother. As Dr. Maté describes it, such a scenario could hypothetically lead the child to conclude several things — each of which is extremely threatening: that there is something wrong with my parents, my parents are bad, my parents don't love me, or that my parents are incompetent, or unhinged, or even that the entire world is unhinged, unpredictable, and unsafe.

All of those options are unendurably threatening to the child — and so, as Dr. Maté explains, we are wired to reject them and select another option. Rather than concluding "my parents are bad" or "my parents are incompetent" or that "the world is unpredictable, arbitrary, and unsafe," we default instead to "there must be something wrong with *me*." While this conclusion is traumatic, in that it by its divides us against ourselves, it is less terrifying than the alternative. As Dr. Maté points out, this position leaves the child with something that they can try to address: they can try to change *themselves*, they can try to become "good enough." The other options leave the child powerless: this option enables the child to try to do something, change something, fix something, in order to try to fix the terrifying situation.

Note that Dr. Heller's statement is telling us very much the same thing: the child is programmed to see himself or herself as "bad," in order to see the parent as "good," because the child depends upon the parent for its very survival. Thus, Dr. Heller explains, the child responds by turning against the Self. If the parent is "bad," there is nothing the child can do about it, but if we turn on ourselves, he says, we can try to "make ourselves better" and preserve the hope that we can "win love."

While this coping mechanism may strike us as regrettable and mistaken, the fact is that as a child we simply have no choice: the decision to turn on ourselves is not actually a decision or a choice at all, but rather an automatic and unavoidable response which is hard-wired into us whether we like it or not. As Dr. Maté explains elsewhere:

> If our environment cannot support our gut feelings and our emotions then the child, in order to "belong" and "fit in" will automatically, unwittingly and unconsciously, suppress their emotions and their connections to themselves, for the sake of staying connected to the nurturing environment, without which the child cannot survive. [. . .] Automatically, we disconnect from ourselves, in order to continue to be looked after. It's a tragic choice. It's not even a choice — the child's

not aware of making a choice. It's an automatic process. Then we get into adulthood, and all of a sudden we say, "I don't know who I am." Especially people in mid-life — they realize that they've been living lives that were not their own lives at all. They did it all because they got disconnected.[69]

And it is exactly *this* tragic aspect of our human nature and wiring, I argue, that is being dramatized in so many of the world's ancient myths — including the story of Peter betraying Jesus and saying several times, "I never knew him!"

Clearly such a psychological injury, sufficient to cause us to suppress Self and disconnect from who we really are, must be extremely painful and damaging. Some psychologists use the term "attachment injury" for such circumstances in which a child's necessary attachment to a parent or primary caregiver — an attachment which is a matter of survival for the child — leads to this type of internal disconnection within the child, following the pioneering work of psychologists John Bowlby (1907 — 1990) and Mary Ainsworth (1913 – 1999) who studied among other evidence the impact of separation on children from their parents during World War II and among orphans and other displaced children during the war and afterwards.

In a 1973 study entitled *Attachment and Loss,* Bowlby argues that a child is wired for its very survival to be attached to its caregiver figure (commonly the parents), and that separation from the caregiver, or even indifference from the caregiver (let alone actual rejection by the caregiver), causes extreme anxiety in the child and leads eventually to the development of unhealthy anger, fears and phobias. Noting that the significance of attachment had generally been overlooked by psychologists (with some exceptions, including the observant William James at the end of the 19th century), Bowlby writes: "no fear-arousing situation is missed or camouflaged as often as is fear that an attachment figure will be inaccessible or unresponsive."[70]

Richard Schwartz has found that the impact of attachment injury resulting in feelings of abandonment, rejection, betrayal, shame, fear, inadequacy, unworthiness leads the parts who comprise our internal family to reject and suppress the Self, and to try to bury and suppress those heartbreaking feelings as well. As Dr. Schwartz explains, the most sensitive parts in the internal system will generally be the ones who, most severely impacted by those hurts, will carry them around like a painful, heavy burden — and the other parts will shun and isolate the burden-carrying part or parts, turning them into an exile, avoided and rejected by the rest of the internal family.

In *No Bad Parts*, he writes of these exiles:

> Before we get hurt, they are the delightful, playful, creative, trusting, innocent, and open parts of us that we love to be close to. They are also the most sensitive parts, so when someone hurts, betrays, shames, or scares us, they are the parts who take in the extreme beliefs and emotions (burdens) from those events the most. After the trauma or attachment injury, the burdens these parts absorb shift them from their fun, playful states to chronically wounded inner children who are frozen in the past and have the ability to overwhelm us and pull us back into those dreadful scenes. They move from feeling "I am loved" to "I am worthless" and "No one loves me," and when they blend with us, that belief becomes our

paradigm and we feel all their burdened emotions. [. . .] This is why we try our best to lock these parts away, thinking that we are simply moving on from bad memories, sensations, and emotions — not realizing that we are disconnecting from our most precious resources just because they got hurt.[71]

An exile in our inner family is carrying a tremendous burden — a rucksack full of pain from an ancient injury, often from a wounding that happened during childhood and in relation to a parent or beloved caregiver whom we loved and trusted and to whom we were attached. That pain and heartbreak is so toxic that the other parts don't want it around: it's like a backpack full of radioactive material that needs to be locked away in a lead-lined vault behind thick strongroom doors.

This internal division and separation resulting in the isolation of exiles manifests outwardly in what John Bowlby called *detachment*. Writing in the same 1973 book cited earlier, and drawing on observations he and Mary Ainsworth made over the course of decades, Bowlby explains that our response to attachment injury follows an arc from *protest*, to *despair*, to *detachment*, and that all three are must be viewed as "phases of a single process" resulting ultimately in a failure to even "recognize," much less respond to, the parent-figure.[72] The sensitive, trusting, childlike parts who are forced to bear the pain of betrayal and heartbreak have now been transformed and locked away — resulting in a rejection of the very attachment that led to the heartbreak, as a severe form of self-defense in the wake of the injury. Bowlby notes that these stages of protest, despair and detachment may be more muted in older children or adolescents than in children who are younger when the attachment injury occurs, but that they are present nonetheless.[73]

The internal division and detachment, in other words, spreads outward to the world, like ripples spreading outward in a pond from the splash of a single pebble. In a quotation that I am fond of citing, one of the pioneering psychologists to devote his practice to the understanding and healing of trauma, Dr. Peter Levine, starkly and concisely describes this outwardly-cascading aspect of trauma and separation: "In short, trauma is about loss of connection — to ourselves, to our bodies, to our families, to others, and to the world around us."[74]

For those who find illustrations from movies to be helpful in demonstrating these effects, I would suggest the character of Zach Mayo in the 1982 film, *An Officer and a Gentleman*. In that movie, we are shown a series of flashbacks that Zach has suffered from trauma as a young child, including the death of his mother by suicide and the absence of his father who is an enlisted chief petty officer in the US Navy, often away on months-long cruises onboard Navy vessels, and unsuited by his own admission to being a father to Zach. The movie also implies that Zach's father is probably an alcoholic.

The events of the film dramatize Zach's self-imposed detachment and disconnection, including more than one point in the movie in which he expresses, sometimes vehemently, his rejection of close relationships. During one particularly painful scene, when Zach's girlfriend Paula Pokrifki tells him she loves him and tries to comfort him after the suicide of his friend Sid Worley, Zach yells: "No! I don't want you to love me! I don't want anyone to love me! I just want OUT!"[75]

The disconnection that Dr. Peter Levine describes separates us from others in the human family, and mirrors the separation that takes place inside of us as a result of trauma.

The world's ancient myths and folktales are replete with examples dramatizing the isolation of exiles, such as the many different variations on stories in which a dangerous giant is locked away in a tower behind a door bolted with seven locks. Sometimes, instead of a giant, it is a lonely princess who is locked behind the door of seven locks. In either case, the door is almost certainly the constellation Ophiuchus, whose similarity to both a tower and to a door is self-evident and has been pointed out in many of my previous explanations of specific myths from around the world.

The seven locks of the door could either be the multiple heads of the constellation Scorpio (immediately below Ophiuchus), which often appears in myth as a multi-headed serpent (sometimes with seven heads, sometimes with eight, sometimes with nine, and even occasionally with ten), or they could have to do with the arc-shaped constellation Corona Borealis, which is a bright and beautiful constellation composed of a curve of seven stars just over the "serpent's head" section of Ophiuchus. Perhaps the seven stars of Corona Borealis are seven keys dangling on an arc-shaped key-ring, to unlock the seven locks represented by Scorpio (or vice versa). In any case, this recurring pattern can certainly be seen to be representative of what Richard Schwartz has observed to be true of the locking away of the exiles that can happen within our own internal system.

Among the most revealing of all the ancient stories dramatizing the condition and characteristics of the exile must certainly be the famous myth of Medusa. In the Theogony attributed to Hesiod, we read that Medusa's fate was a sad one (or that she "suffered painfully"), and that she was once a mortal woman (unlike the other Gorgons), after which the poem then immediately says that the Dark-Haired One (meaning the sea-god Poseidon) lay with her among the spring flowers.[76]

Left unsaid in the Theogony is whether that union was voluntary or whether Medusa was raped by the god, but the myth of Medusa was well-known and often-mentioned in other ancient texts, and the discussion of Medusa in the Metamorphoses of the ancient Roman poet Ovid (43 BC – AD 17 or 18) makes it clear that she was raped, and that her transformation into a terrifying monster took place after that rape, and as a result of it.

In the Metamorphoses, we read that Medusa was once a beautiful young woman, of whom many suitors dreamed of marrying and for whose hand many young men contended, and that her most famous feature was her luxurious hair. But, Ovid continues, she was ravished or violated or raped by the god Poseidon in the temple of the goddess Athena (Ovid uses the Roman names Neptune and Minerva for the god of the sea and the goddess of wisdom).[77]

Ovid then tells us (in the original Latin): *neve hoc inpune fuisset, Gorgoneum crinem turpes mutavit in hydros* — literally, "so that this which happened should not go without punishment, the Gorgon's hair she [the goddess Athena] transformed into hideous water-serpents."[78]

In other words, the goddess Athena, outraged by the rape of Medusa within the temple of Athena, decrees that the deed shall not go unpunished, and transforms Medusa's hair into serpents (implying that this is the point at which the famously beautiful, widely pursued and desirable young woman was changed into a deadly monster).

Upon learning of this sequence of events, the modern reader might well find their sensibilities offended, exclaiming: "Wait! What? How is that fair? Medusa was the one who is raped, and then she is also the one who is punished? I don't understand!"

But the ancient myths are not about depicting for us what is "fair" — instead, they are dramatizing profound truths about ourselves, truths which are vitally important for us to understand. It is exactly through such traumatic, shame-inducing events as rape and other forms of violation that innocent and benevolent and happy parts within our internal family become exiles, transformed from beauty and happiness into despair, misery, and isolation — their frightful burden now so toxic that it carries with it a dreadful power which seems impossible to face.

Now, instead of being flocked with suitors contending for her hand in marriage, Medusa will end up exiled to an island with the other two monstrous Gorgons — a lonely island whose location is described in the Theogony as being beyond the great world-encircling Ocean-stream, in the uttermost place, on the fringe of endless night.[79]

This dramatic transformation, from a beautiful and naturally innocent young woman to a deadly monster with toxic petrifying gaze, reveals a vital lesson for our understanding, if we can only see and hear what the myths are trying to show us and tell us. We can be quite certain that the story of Medusa depicts for us the transformation that Dr. Schwartz describes of innocent parts who are forced to become exiles, and we can see that in the story by the very fact that Medusa, once transformed, is then sequestered on an island so remote that it is nearly impossible to find. In fact, in the ancient stories about Medusa, the hero Perseus must first undertake a difficult journey to the mysterious entities known as the Phorkides (daughters of Phorkys, a deep sea-god) or the Graeae (also spelled *Graiai*, the "old women" or the "grey sisters"), just to learn the way to the island where Medusa has been banished, so remote and forlorn is the location of that isle.

This fact in and of itself reveals something to us about our exiles which is worth contemplating carefully: in order to even reach them, we may have to "get through the defense" posed by other parts, who have taken up "protector" roles to shield the location of our banished exiles. But another important piece of evidence which helps confirm the conclusion that Medusa represents our exiles is the fact that this transformation, from beautiful maiden into toxic monster, matches the experience Dr. Richard Schwartz describes regarding the role of exile parts, based on his interactions with thousands of men and women.

In the chapter describing exiles in his book *No Bad Parts*, Dr. Schwartz describes the transformation by which exiled parts can become extreme and frightening. Schwartz quotes poet and author Robert Bly (1926 – 2001), who himself explored myth and folklore for inspiration and used folkloric figures in his books including *Iron John*, describing parts of ourself who "our parents don't like" being pushed into an "invisible bag" which is then sealed up — and the transformation that takes place when those parts are exiled. Bly writes:

> When we put a part of ourselves in the bag it regresses. It de-evolves toward barbarism. Suppose a young man seals a bag at twenty and then waits fifteen or twenty years before he opens it again. What will he find? Sadly, the sexuality, the wildness, the impulsiveness, the anger, the freedom he put in have all regressed; they are not only primitive in mood, they are hostile to the person who opens the bag. The man who opens his bag at forty-five or the woman who opens her bag rightly feels fear.[80]

The passage which Dr. Schwartz cites in the above quotation from Robert Bly is from Bly's 1988 publication, *A Little Book on the Human Shadow*, and it is part of Robert Bly's discussion in that book about a famous story by Scottish author Robert Louis Stevenson (1850 – 1894), *The Strange Case of Dr. Jekyll and Mr. Hyde* (1886). As Robert Bly interprets this story, the kind and caring and good-natured Dr. Jekyll, "always thinking of the good of others," has banished certain parts of himself to that "invisible bag" — "and the substance in the bag takes on a personality of its own; it can't be ignored."[81]

Emerging sporadically from that place of banishment, the exiled part of Dr. Jekyll goes on night-time binges in the city in the shape of Mr. Hyde, sometimes committing acts of violence and brutality and ultimately a murder. Bly observes that if we don't go down and face these exiles, if we try to be (in his words) "shadow-haters," we will end up in the same position as Dr. Jekyll, "with a monkey-like Mr. Hyde scurrying among back buildings elsewhere in the city."[82]

It is the exiles, with their toxic burdens of trauma and the fear they inspire in the parts who take up protecting roles as managers and firefighters (to keep the exiles from being triggered and re-emerging), which drive the discord and division of the whole internal landscape. Just as the goddess Eris triggers first disharmony amongst the family of the gods and then disharmony among the kingdoms of mortal men and women, leading to the conflagration of the Trojan War, it is the exiles and their exclusion from the internal family which leads to the polarization of the rest of the parts, bringing polarization and interior battles as violent as those described in the ancient epic of Troy.

In fact, near the beginning of his latest book *Introduction to Internal Family Systems* (2023), after describing examples of behaviors and thought patterns which several of his clients were struggling with when they came to him, Dr. Schwartz actually uses the phrase "at war" to describe their inner landscapes, saying: "All the people I have described in this chapter came to me at war with themselves."[83]

As the quotations above from Robert Bly make clear, and as Richard Schwartz explains in his own writings, the tactic of sending the most sensitive and innocent members of our internal family off to a lonely island or locked cell in a tower does not work very well (although it basically happens without any conscious decision as a result of attachment injury and trauma). Those exiles become terrifying, and even though they are unseen, their power (and the toxic effects of the burdens that they carry) is such that they disrupt the entire internal family, causing our other parts to take up roles which they too may dislike but which are forced upon them again without much conscious consideration, as a form of internal systemic defense. These roles often create internal polarization in which parts line up on either side of the battlefield, just as the gods and goddesses in the Iliad choose sides in the Trojan War based on their own hurts and passions.

But the good news is that exiles can be transformed and brought back into the community of the internal family, laying down and de-fusing their former burdens — and that when they are transformed, the other parts who have taken on often-unwelcome roles in an attempt to isolate and quarantine those exiles can also walk away from their own negative roles and find a less unwelcome way to contribute to the internal family.

In fact, "transform" is the very word that Dr. Schwartz uses again and again to describe what happens when exiles are faced and their burdens are dealt with. In *No Bad Parts*, he says in various places:

"Parts are thrust into given roles and they long to be released from them. Once they are free, they transform."[84]

"Listening to, embracing, and loving parts allows them to heal and transform as much as it does for people. In Buddhist terms, IFS helps peoples become bodhisattvas of their psyches in the sense of helping each inner sentient being (part) become enlightened through compassion and love."[85]

"Going to war against protector parts only makes them stronger. Listening to them and loving them, however, helps them heal and transform."[86]

"As soon as burdens leave parts' bodies, parts immediately transform into their original, valuable states. It's as if a curse was lifted from an inner Sleeping Beauty, or ogre, or addict."[87]

The final quotation in that list of assertions about parts being transformed as burdens are lifted references fairy tale parallels such as Sleeping Beauty coming out from under the curse (which also, in the original story, impacted her entire family and indeed all who lived within her castle), or an ogre being transformed back into a person. And, in the story of Medusa, we find a similar kind of transformation taking place, once Perseus learns from Athena and Hermes how he can face Medusa without having to fear her dreadful petrifying power.

To be sure, the "transformation" of the exiled Medusa involves her having her head cut off by Perseus, but this aspect of the story (as with most aspects of ancient myths around the world) can be definitively shown to be based on the arrangements of the constellations themselves — and the larger point for our examination of the transformation of exiles is that, out of the neck of the slain Medusa emerges the beautiful winged horse Pegasus, flying upwards like a symbol of liberation and power and exultation. The ancient texts also tell us that a powerful youth named Chrysaor, whose name means "golden blade," emerges from the neck of Medusa along with Pegasus.

The fact is that we cannot "kill" or "get rid of" any of our parts — nor should we want to, once we understand that each is a vital living being, given to us for our blessing, with resources and gifts we need in our life, and yet prone to taking on unwelcome roles and behaviors due to events in our past which wound us, and the pain of which we continue to carry. Thus, if Medusa dramatizes for us the characteristics of parts who are forced to become exiles (and I think the evidence is absolutely conclusive that she does), then we must understand the mission of Perseus in a different way than simply "slaying" Medusa.

As hinted already, there is much that we can learn from the myth of Perseus and Medusa which can help us in discovering and dealing with our exiles (and with the disharmony that the presence of these exiles, with their toxic burdens, inevitably create in our own internal landscape). The first lesson is that we must approach exiles in a Self-led manner. In the story of Perseus and Medusa, as I spend some time discussing in *Myth and Trauma*, young Perseus is goaded into agreeing to the mission of bringing back the head of Medusa. The conniving king of the island where Perseus and his mother Danaë have been living wants to sleep with Danaë, but Perseus has grown into a formidable young man and can protect his mother from the king's unwelcome advances. So the king of the island appeals to the youthful pride of Perseus and gets the young man to agree to go and do what so many have previously attempted and failed: bring back the head of Medusa.

Perseus starts out in high spirits and full of confidence in his strength and prowess, little knowing what he is really getting into. He appears to have agreed to the mission without actual awareness of the dangerous ability of Medusa to turn men to stone. As I argue in *Myth and Trauma*, this power to turn anyone who sees her into a stone statue can be interpreted metaphorically as the ability to turn us into an *object*, taking away our agency and *subjective* power, just as the triggering of our exiles and the re-surfacing of the deep burdens and heartbreaks that they are carrying can cause us to act (or, more accurately, *react*) in ways we later regret, as if we have been taken over by some foreign force — in other words, enslaving us to unwelcome patterns of behavior as if a computer virus has taken over our operating system, robbing us of agency and making us react like an automaton whose "buttons have been pushed" and who can only carry out its programming, making us an *object* instead of a subject.

The ancient sources tell us, however, that Perseus is visited by the gods — specifically Athena and Hermes — and that through their assistance, he receives guidance that will enable him to carry out his mission successfully. They inform Perseus of the powers of the three Gorgons, and instruct him of the proper way to approach them so that he will not be turned to stone. They also inform him that in order to even find the forlorn island where Medusa dwells with the other two Gorgons, Perseus must make his way to the remote home of the Graeae. In different versions of the story which have survived from ancient writers, Perseus must sometimes learn from them where to find still further Nymphs who will give him some of the tools that he will need in his quest, such as winged sandals, and the adamantine blade with which to cut through the neck of Medusa, and the *kibisis* pouch in which he can safely carry her head, while in other versions Perseus receives these important items from the gods Hermes and Athena themselves.

In either case, the important point is that Perseus cannot confidently and safely approach the exile — cannot even find the exile, in fact — without the help of the gods, at least one of whom, Athena, can be shown beyond doubt to be associated with Ophiuchus, the constellation which so often portrays aspects of our Self in the myths. Some of the aspects of Athena which give us confidence in knowing that she is associated with Ophiuchus include the fact that she is said to spring full-grown and already carrying her famous spear from the head of her father Zeus, the fact that a spear is her chosen weapon, and the fact that she is almost always depicted and described as wearing a long, full-length robe, sometimes one that is fringed with serpents (when fringed with serpents, this robe is the famous Aegis).

All of these details can be confidently associated with the figure of Ophiuchus, which is located immediately below the constellation Hercules, which we have already seen to represent the god Zeus, from whose head Athena leaps full-grown:

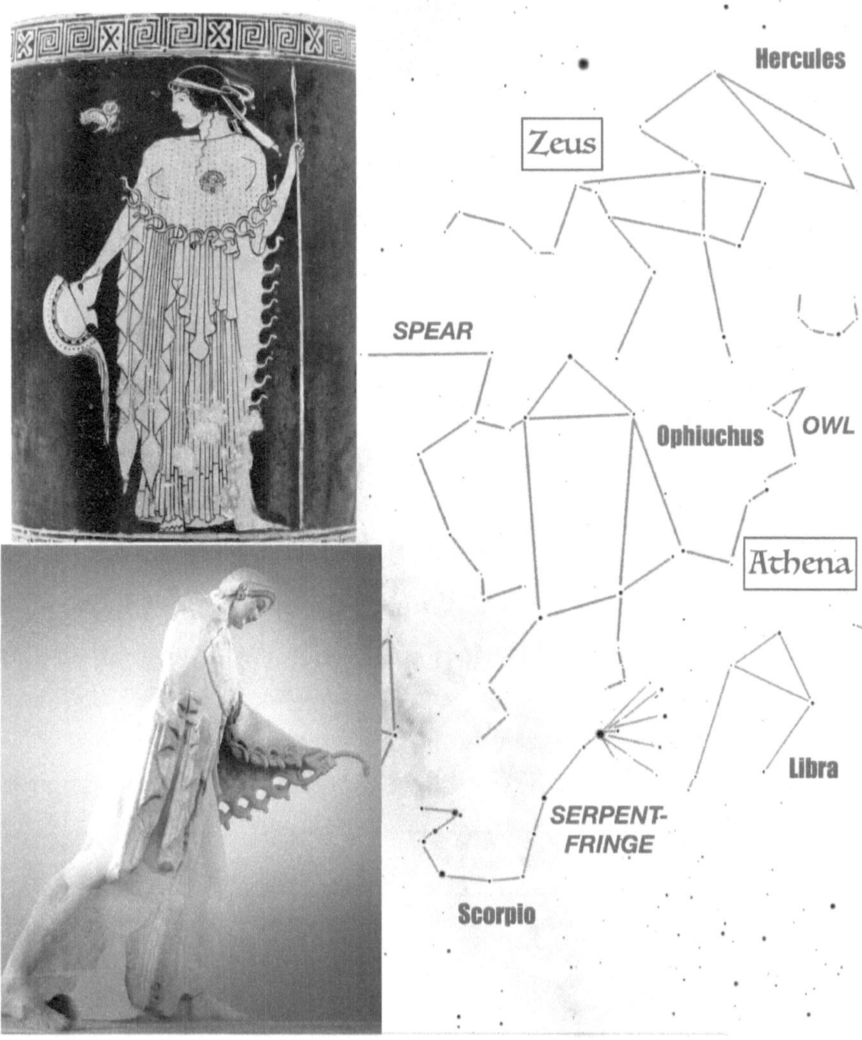

We can see in the above images from ancient depictions of the goddess Athena her long narrow tunic, fringed with serpents — and compare their shape and outline to the oblong central body of Ophiuchus, just above the "serpent-fringed" figure of Scorpio. We can also see how the two "halves" of the serpent held by Ophiuchus can be envisioned as a spear, particularly the "tail" side of the serpent, on the left of the outline of the constellation shown above and labeled "Spear" in the image, although in some other examples from ancient myth, figures associated with Ophiuchus will even carry two spears (as does Hector, in the Iliad, who can also confidently be associated with Ophiuchus). Sometimes, instead of a spear, a figure associated with Ophiuchus will carry a staff or rod, as does Moses in the Bible stories (and note of course that the staff or rod of Moses turns into a serpent on more than one occasion, which adds further evidence for the connection between his staff and the "serpent" held by the constellation Ophiuchus).

Additionally, in one of the images above, the goddess is shown accompanied by an owl, a bird associated with the goddess of wisdom. I have elsewhere noted that the roughly triangular "serpent's head" of Ophiuchus could perhaps be seen as very similar to the facial features of an owl, which may explain this association of the goddess with this specific night-hunting bird. The diagram above labels the serpent-head side of the constellation with the word "Owl."

Note in the ancient vase-painting shown above, the owl is depicted on the side of the goddess that is opposite to the side with the spear, although the image "reverses" the sides we might expect to find the spear and the owl. In other words, in the sky, the "spear" is on the left side of the constellation, and the "owl" is on the right, when the triangular "head" of the constellation is facing "up" and the two feet are facing down (in other words, as an observer in the northern hemisphere would see the constellation, when facing towards the south). In the ancient artwork, the spear is instead depicted as being on the right and the owl as being on the left, but note that the feet of the goddess in the ancient vase-painting are pointing the opposite direction as the feet of the constellation in the star-chart, which indicates that the artist has exercised a bit of artistic license and "reversed" the painting. If we were to simply flip the image left and right, the feet of the goddess in the artwork would point in the same direction as the feet of the constellation in the chart, and the spear would then be on the left side of Athena, and the owl would be above her shoulder on the right. In that case, we might even speculate that the helmet of the goddess, held in her lower hand (below the owl) might correspond to the location of the constellation Libra in the heavens.

In any case, the above should be abundant evidence to confirm that the goddess Athena is associated with Ophiuchus in the heavens. Additional confirmation is found in the fact that she is a goddess of wisdom, and that other figures associated with Ophiuchus (such as King Solomon in the Bible or Odin in the Norse myths) are also associated with wisdom.

Additionally, the goddess Athena is associated with the olive tree, which she gives to the city of Athens as a gift in a mythical account in which the city chooses Athena as its namesake and patron deity. In many previous books and in my online courses about the celestial foundations of the Bible, I have shown that the outline of the constellation Hercules can alternately be envisioned in a "whirling" form, in which the square-shaped head of Hercules becomes a kind of central hub, out of which whirling arms radiate in four directions. This whirling form of the constellation Hercules can be seen to resemble a tree, particularly trees with rather "scraggly" appearance such as fig trees and olive trees — and the constellation Hercules definitely plays the role of a fig tree in the Bible and in the story of the Buddha meditating under the sacred fig, as well as in the Odyssey. In the image below, we see how Athena could be envisioned as holding up or "giving" the olive tree, if the "whirling" form of Hercules is envisioned as a tree:

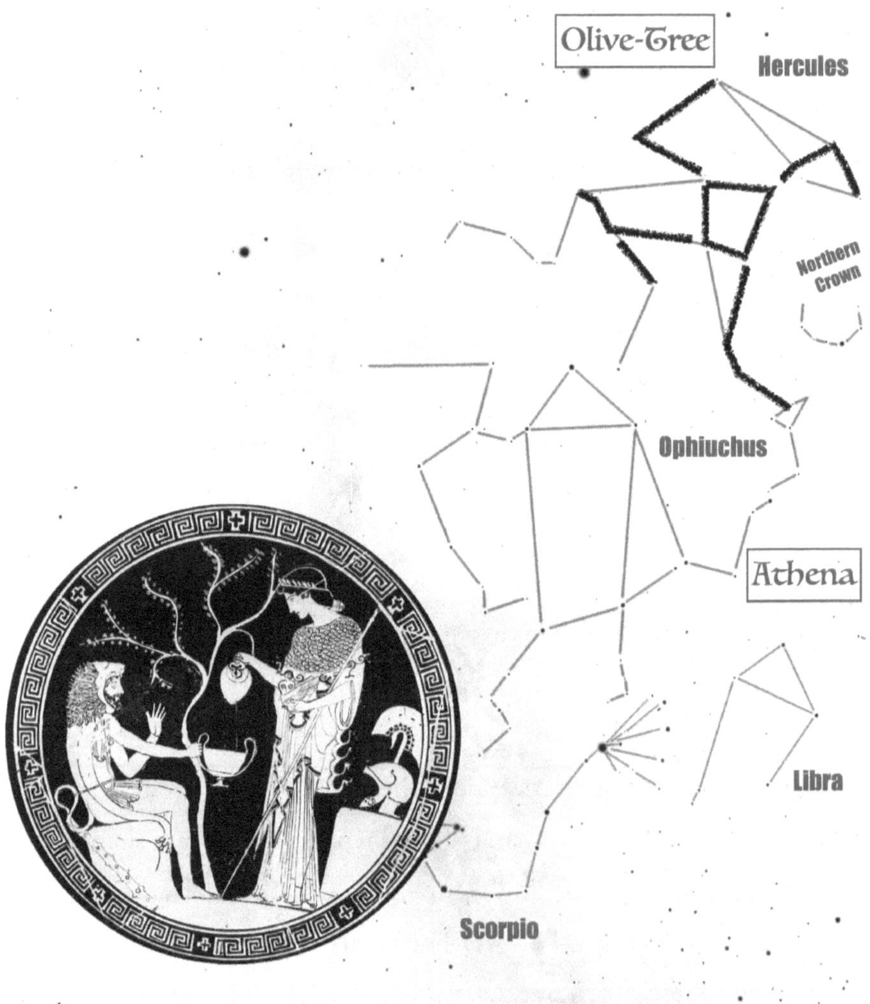

In the image above, I have added in thicker lines the outline of the "whirling" form of the constellation Hercules, and extended one of those lines to the "serpent's head" portion of the constellation Ophiuchus. We can see how the whirling outline could be imagined to resemble a tree, particularly a fig tree or an olive tree, and how in the myth of Athena giving the olive tree as a blessing to the people of the city of Athens we could even imagine the goddess herself (in the figure of Ophiuchus) holding the tree and presenting it as a gift.

I have also included an intriguing (and very artistically beautiful) image showing Athena with the hero Heracles, with a tree between them. The hero Heracles (or Hercules) is of course associated with the constellation Hercules, but I argue that so is this tree! In the artwork, Athena has a rather triangular-looking vase in her upraised hand, with which she is going to pour wine for the hero: I would argue that this again corresponds to the rather triangular "serpent's head" in the constellation itself (and note that it is again opposite to the arm in which she cradles her spear, at an angle, corresponding to the "serpent's tail").

The hero Heracles in this artwork is holding out a double-handled wine-cup to receive the wine from the goddess. It is a type of wine-cup called a *kantharos* or a *cantharus*, in the lexicon of names given to various vessels used in ancient Greece. Note the curved or even arc-shaped outline of this wine-cup, which the artist has emphasized, in the outstretched hand of the hero. Figures associated with the constellation Hercules often grasp a curved or arc-shaped object in their outstretched hand, which I have for years argued (supported by an abundance of compelling evidence from myths around the world, including Bible stories but also myths from the Polynesian cultures of the Pacific, a world away from the Mediterranean Sea) can be explained by the fact that the constellation Corona Borealis (the Northern Crown) is located just in front of the outstretched arm of the constellation Hercules (when the constellation is envisioned in its other outline, as a powerful figure with a square-shaped head, brandishing a weapon overhead with one hand and reaching forward with the other). What is intriguing about this particular depiction of the hero Heracles and the goddess Athena is that the ancient artist has included *both* aspects of the constellation Hercules: one as a powerful human figure with a square-shaped head (made even more square by the lion-skin head-dress that Heracles usually wears), in this case grasping an arc-shaped item in one outstretched hand, *but also* as a tree with branches radiating in all directions!

From all of this discussion, we can see beyond any doubt that the goddess Athena, goddess of wisdom, is associated with Ophiuchus — the very constellation which plays the role of our higher Self in the myths of the world: the very constellation who forms the conduit or linkage through whom receive divine inspiration. She is the one throughout the Odyssey who most often appears to Odysseus and inspires his mind or warns him against rash indiscretion, although (as with the story of Perseus) the god Hermes, messenger of the gods and guide of our immortal soul according to the ancient myths, also appears to guide and to warn Odysseus on occasion as well.

The lesson for us should be clear: approaching an exile must be done with discretion, and guided by the divine inspiration available to us through higher Self. And, as mentioned previously, the details of the story, in which Perseus is first guided by the advice of Athena and Hermes to seek out the Graeae or Phorkides (who in some versions of the tale are actually sisters of the Gorgons, and perhaps of Medusa herself as well) may well be interpreted as dramatizing to us the importance of approaching the various protector parts (managers and firefighters) who have taken up roles to sequester and quarantine the exile and all the heartbreak that the exile carries as a burden. These lessons match to an absolutely astonishing degree the recommendations that Dr. Schwartz and Internal Family Systems therapy give regarding our approach to our exiles, based on tens of thousands of interaction with actual men and women struggling with internal disharmony and exiles who carry burdens of trauma and attachment injury.

Another striking application of the story of Perseus and Medusa which can help us in approaching our own exiles can be seen in the way that, equipped with the gifts provided to him by Athena and Hermes, Perseus no longer need fear the otherwise-terrifying power of Medusa to turn mortals to stone. As mentioned before, the exact details of who gives what gift to Perseus do vary from one ancient account to another, but it is generally understood that the polished and mirror-like shield with which Perseus can safely see Medusa without falling victim to her power of petrification belongs to Athena, and is loaned to the hero by her. Likewise, the winged sandals with which Perseus is able to fly to the remote island of the Gorgons, and then make his escape from the other two sisters after he slays Medusa, are obviously associated with Hermes, and in many versions of the myth are loaned to Perseus by the messenger-god.

In the story, Perseus uses these and other divine gifts in order to safely approach Medusa in order to slay her, but as already noted, we cannot actually "slay" any of our parts, nor should we ever desire to do, once we understand that they can be healed and unburdened of their toxic baggage and released from unwelcome roles in order to again play positive and welcome roles as part of our internal team. Trying to slay or banish or "get rid" of parts only leads to bigger problems and to greater disharmony and polarization within our internal system. The lesson of these various divine gifts, I would argue, is that through Self we have access to all the tools we need to face whatever terrors we may think are lurking in the darkest and most remote corners of our internal landscape.

This aspect of the myth conforms to an absolutely vital and life-changing observation which Dr. Schwartz offers based upon his work with so many men and women. He explains:

There's nothing inside of you that has any power if you are in Self and not afraid of it. This law has also never been proven false in the decades I've been doing this work, and keep in mind that I have worked with clients who have parts that are extremely intimidating and are even determined to hurt or kill them or someone else. And then we do our work together and parts that clients have been afraid of most of their life — parts that feel like actual monsters or demons — suddenly can't do anything to them. The part's usual attempts to control or intimidate now seem feeble, because the client sees what the part is all about, and they see how that part had been stuck in a role.[88]

Thus, I would argue that an important lesson of the Medusa myth might be best stated by saying that with the gifts we receive through Self (our conduit to divine inspiration, clarity, courage and the ability to face any situation), we see that the previously terrifying and objectifying power of our exiles and their burdens need no longer terrify us. Accompanied by Athena, Perseus can approach Medusa safely, and the result is that the old monster is replaced by a beautiful winged horse named Pegasus and a beautiful youth named Chrysaor. We don't necessarily know into who or what our exiles will transform, and the result may surprise us, but in this story the beings who emerge are beautiful and youthful and powerful.

So, how do we begin down the path of healing our exiles and enabling them to release their toxic burdens and find new and more desirable ways to contribute to our internal family? First, I would suggest consulting books by Dr. Schwartz and other IFS practitioners directly, as well as seeing a professional if possible. Our Self is certainly capable of knowing the way and healing our parts, no matter how badly they have been traumatized — but there are obviously a number of advantages to seeking the help of experienced and well-trained healers who have chosen the path of therapy as their life's work and who have been exposed to the internal dynamics of others and become familiar with them.

That said, I am also convinced that the precious treasure that all cultures have been given in the form of the world's ancient myths stand ready to guide us and that these sacred stories constitute a tremendous resource for our benefit in this life, and that we must not underestimate the power they have to offer to us. As the myth of Perseus shows us, we must first approach the protectors who guard the way to our exiles, and if we hope to be successful in our quest, we must do so guided by Self rather than by any of the impulsive motives which betoken the presence of compensating parts. In the story, Perseus is able to bargain with the Graeae, and get them to promise to help him — and in his work with thousands of clients, Dr. Schwartz similarly reports that when we ask our various parts to promise not to overwhelm us and to give us space so that we can find out what is going on and how we can help, they will actually honor that contract once they have committed to such an agreement.

Often, protectors will operate in pairs to protect an exile, and these pro-tectors will often become polarized against one another to some degree. For example, imagine an exile who is bearing a burden of pain because one of the child's parents conveyed some form of the message: "You will never amount to anything," or "You can't do anything right." Such a message can be conveyed by a parent either verbally or through other non-verbal means, but either way it can create a tremendous burden of shame, insecurity, and lack of confidence for the child which can persist into adulthood and result in self-sabotaging behavior which makes the hurtful message into a kind of self-fulfilling prophecy.

The protector parts who take up the job of trying to keep that heartbreaking burden from surfacing may try different and even opposing tactics to try to keep the exile who is carrying that heartbreak from crossing the stage of our conscious mind. One part may take on a "manager" role, trying to be perfect, pleasing others excessively in an attempt to overcome the message (which one of the parts is still carrying) of "You'll never amount to anything" or "You can't do anything right." This part may drive the individual to rack up accomplishments in the eyes of the world, such as college degrees from prestigious institutions or increasingly lucrative positions of responsibility within the corporate world, but deep down the individual is still tormented by the humiliating, critical voice of the parent who conveyed the heartbreaking message to the child that he or she was "no good" and would never measure up. The exiled part who is bearing this terrible burden must be kept from being triggered, and the managerial part takes on a desperate role to accomplish something that will silence that voice, but to no avail: the critical message (perhaps even in the voice of the parent who first conveyed it, or perhaps in some new, twisted inner voice belonging to the lonely exile) will still flash across the internal landscape at the most inconvenient moments, triggering an avalanche of emotions and feelings of worthlessness and self-loathing.

Because the manager part will never be able to accomplish enough to leave aside that childhood burden of unworthiness conveyed by the parent or caregiver, it will often be accompanied by another part using an entirely different tactic to help dull the pain of the hurtful toxic burden carried by the exile in question. For example, a different part may take on a "firefighter" role, ready to swoop in an douse the pain of the worthlessness message that the inner child is carrying. In some individuals, this firefighter may try to douse the pain with a bout of heavy drinking, in others the tactic used might be very different — but note that the managerial part who is trying to keep the worthlessness voice at bay through tactics of people-pleasing or trophy-gathering may well resent the firefighter part who swoops in to drown the pain using a bottle of alcohol, just as the firefighter part may well resent the managerial part whose people-pleasing never actually "works" to the degree that the manager hopes it will. Thus, the exile, the manager, and the firefighter form a kind of "polarized triangle" within the inner landscape, whipsawing the grown child with sudden storms or inner battles that will never be stilled until the burden itself is resolved.

From experience, we know that almost anything can trigger these internal flareups. For example, in the scenario above in which the child received the heartbreaking message from a parent or caregiver that "You're no good — you can't do anything right — you'll never amount to anything," something as simple as dropping a spoon on the floor while emptying the dishwasher (even in an empty house, with no one else to witness the dropped spoon) might trigger the exile who is bearing the burden, causing that exile to waddle across the front stage of the mind carrying the exile's heavy rucksack of toxic self-criticism. The manager part, who spends all its time in the thankless (and Sisyphean) task of trying to do everything right, is horrified at the sight of the exile and aghast to hear that withering voice from the past repeating, "See! You're hopeless!"

The firefighter part, who looks down on the manager and who is in turn despised by the manager, then comes flying across the stage to try and contain the damage, perhaps spraying alcohol everywhere in an attempt to "put out the fire" of heartbreak (never mind the consequences tomorrow or the long-term health impact of repeated binges), or perhaps using another tactic. Other firefighter tactics which parts may use instead of substance abuse might be fits of rage, which can also be seen as an attempt to try and contain the exile and get the exile back off the stage and into its place of isolation. If I drop a spoon while emptying the dishwasher and suddenly fly into a fit of rage, I should ask myself what could possibly be going on, that something as simple as a dropped spoon could cause such a reaction. Obviously, the dropped spoon is simply not that important, in and of itself. Presumably, I have a whole drawer full of spoons, and I am in no danger of starving to death for want of a spoon (and, if it is my only spoon and I really need it for my dinner, I can always just wash it off myself, if I drop it on the floor). The dropped spoon has obviously triggered something deeper — a childhood heartbreak or trauma of some sort, which I am still carrying, and the fit of rage is an attempt by a firefighter part to keep that painful message from surfacing, and to contain it again as quickly as possible.

Another possible polarized triangle might feature a managerial part who tries to do everything right and tries to rack up accomplishment after accomplishment in endless attempt to suppress some childhood heartbreak, lined up opposite another part whose strategy is actually to "not try" in any way (we might call it a "slacker" strategy). While it may seem counterintuitive at first, such a tactic might be employed as a safety valve by which the part can say: "See? We didn't fail, because we didn't even try!" Such a strategy actually makes some sense, if the child was given a burden similar to those cited above, in which the message was: "You'll never amount to anything — you fail at everything — you're no good." In a desperate tactic to keep that message from rising up to the surface, the part who has taken on the slacker role tries not to do anything, as a means of never having to fail. Obviously, the managerial part resents the slacker part, and vice versa.

The good news is that exiles can be transformed and harmony restored. As we have already seen, the experience of Dr. Schwartz and other practitioners of IFS, based on interaction with literally tens of thousands of men and women with parts displaying all kinds of unwelcome and sometimes very extreme behavior, is that Self can lead this process, and that Self in fact is absolutely indispensable to this process. It cannot take place without Self: parts can adopt various coping behaviors, but they are not Self and cannot heal other parts, as Self can. And, as we have also already seen, the ancient myths given to humanity thousands of years ago and present in virtually every culture around the globe dramatize this very same truth.

In the Perseus myth, for example, it is very clear that without the guidance of the gods, Perseus could not have safely approached the exiled Medusa. However, Perseus is the son of Zeus and a mortal woman, in a pattern which repeats itself throughout myth around the world, symbolizing the fact that we ourselves, although born of physical mortal matter, also possess a divine spark which comes from a source which cannot be explained through mere material physics — and Perseus is attuned to the inspiration offered by the gods (as those who had unsuccessfully tried to approach Medusa in the past apparently were not). But because he is in contact with Athena and Hermes, Perseus is well equipped to face Medusa and can in fact do so without fear. Many ancient depictions of Perseus facing Medusa in fact show Athena standing beside Perseus:

This ancient illustration is extremely revealing, and all the more so if we understand the set of constellations in the night sky upon which the story of Perseus slaying Medusa can be shown to be based. In this particular piece of artwork, thought to date to around 450 BC and currently in the possession of the Metropolitan Museum of Art in New York City, we see arranged from left to right the goddess Athena, with Perseus in the center looking back over his shoulder as he faces to the right, where a sleeping Medusa is about to be slain by the hero. In other ancient artwork, Perseus slays Medusa and is flanked on either side by both the goddess Athena on one side, and the god Hermes on the other, but in this image we see Athena by herself, and Perseus staring intently into her eyes as he slays Medusa.

The scene of Perseus slaying Medusa can be definitively linked to the region of the sky containing the constellation that bears the hero's name, Perseus. As can be seen in the image below, the constellation Perseus as outlined by H. A. Rey can be seen to be holding a kind of "hook-shaped" implement in the hand on the left of the central body as we face the outline when its feet are oriented downwards and head oriented upwards:

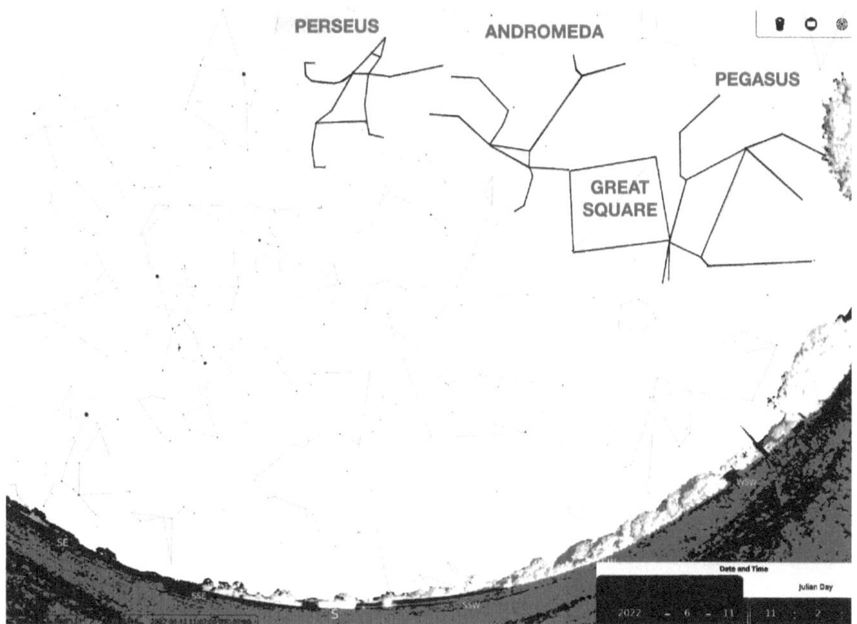

The hero Perseus uses a special hook-shaped sword when he cuts off the head of Medusa, known as the *harpe* sword — and we can see from the actual stars in the night sky why the story (and ancient artwork) specifically has Perseus carry a hook-like sword, due to the hook-shape created by the stars themselves on the left side of the constellation (the east side of the constellation: in the above star-chart, we are in the northern hemisphere and facing towards the south, which is why we see the front foot of the constellation Pegasus on the right starting to disappear behind a tree on the right or western edge of the planetarium screen).

Below are two examples of ancient vases, both showing Perseus and both showing his harpe weapon, on the left side of the body or the head in both illustrations:

From this detail alone, we can be confident that Perseus in the heavens corresponds to Perseus in the myths when he is preparing to slay Medusa, holding his harpe sword in the hand on the eastern side of the constellation (the fact that the constellation itself is named "Perseus" is an additional clue, although not always definitive when it comes to identifying the corresponding constellation in ancient myth).

Now, going back to the previous star-chart, we can see that the constellation Andromeda is basically "laid out" adjacent to the constellation Perseus, on the western side of Perseus (and labelled in the star-chart). Note that the constellation Andromeda itself can be envisioned as not having a head: at the end of the "neck" of the constellation Andromeda we see the Great Square of the constellation Pegasus. The Great Square can be envisioned as one of the mighty wings of the horse Pegasus himself, and we can see the horse-shaped outline of Pegasus on the opposite side of the Great Square from the figure of Andromeda.

In other words, in the layout of the constellations themselves in the night sky, we see the great horse Pegasus emerging "from the neck" of the constellation Andromeda, which is lying next to the constellation Perseus which holds the hooked sword — indicating that Medusa can be confidently associated with the constellation Andromeda when her head is cut off and Pegasus emerges!

What is so intriguing about this identification of both the hero and Medusa is that, in the image from 450 BC now on display in the Met Museum of New York, we see Perseus and Medusa very much in the place and posture of the constellations Perseus and Andromeda in the night sky — but not Athena!

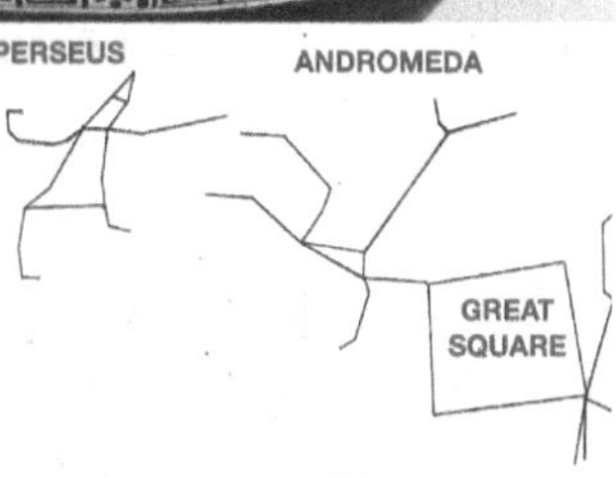

In other words, the ancient artist has very carefully patterned the artwork after the constellations in the night sky, even having the rightward foot of Perseus higher than the left (corresponding to the constellation itself) and angling the body of Medusa in a way which corresponds to the angle of the constellation Andromeda relative to Perseus — but the artist has added the goddess Athena where no corresponding constellation in the sky suggests Athena! We have already seen that the goddess Athena can be confidently identified with the constellation Ophiuchus (a constellation often associated with figures who dramatize the characteristics of higher Self, including both Jesus and the Buddha), but Ophiuchus is not located to the left or east of Perseus in the sky, and the constellations which are located to the left or east of Perseus are not good matches for Athena at all.

The head of Perseus in the constellation can be envisioned as "looking away" from Andromeda, just as Perseus must look away from Medusa when he cuts off her head, so that he is not turned to stone. It is therefore fascinating that the ancient artist has Perseus looking away from Medusa and looking directly towards the goddess of wisdom, as if *she* is guiding his hand!

When we approach our exiles, then, it must be done through Self, and guided by the higher wisdom to which we have access through Self, by virtue of the fact that (like Perseus in the myth) we are children of both matter and spirit, possessed of a divine spark which has been temporarily lodged in a physical body.

In the paradigm of Internal Family Systems, we are advised to approach the *protectors* first, those who are "running interference" for the sequestered exile, and to begin our internal conversation with them. If we are doing this "in Self," we will approach them with compassion and clarity and all the other traits inherent to Self. If we are approaching them with impatience or frustration or anger or fear, we can be certain we are not in Self but rather that there is another part trying to manipulate the situation, and we need to patiently ask that part (and any successive parts) if it would please step aside for a short period of time in order to give us an opportunity to learn more about other parts who need our help.

Envisioning the above image of Perseus looking intently into the eyes of Athena might be a very helpful practice as we proceed with any quest to get to know our exiles in order to heal them and allow them to put down their burdens.

When we are in Self, as opposed to blended with a polarizing part, then we can appreciate the roles that our protectors have taken on, even if their behaviors have not been welcome. We can thank them for what they were trying to do, helping to hold the internal family together as best they could in a difficult situation, and we can confidently tell them that Self can in fact heal the exile and help the exile to let go of the toxic burden in order to transform — and that if the exile can let go of it, that will mean that the protector can find a more welcome role to play as well, instead of always trying to prevent the exile from getting out of quarantine.

Dr. Schwartz describes the process in *No Bad Parts*:

> An exile is healed when Self retrieves it from where it is stuck
> in the past. Then the exile can unburden and begin to rein-
> tegrate with all the other parts in the system. [. . .] Exiles need
> you to connect with them until they trust you. Then they
> need you to witness what happened to them and know how

truly bad it was. Then you can go back to where they are stuck in the past and bring them out. At that point, they are usually willing to unburden the beliefs and emotions they've been carrying.[89]

Remarkably (but not unexpectedly, if Dr. Schwartz is indeed right about what is going on in our internal landscape based on his observations and experience, as I am convinced that he is), the ancient myths dramatize this process and the details in those myths can serve as a tremendous resource help us with our own situation.

In the story of Peter in the gospels with which we started this chapter, after Peter denies ever knowing Jesus, we find an episode which is known as the "restoration of Peter," which has traditionally been interpreted as Jesus restoring the breach that took place in the relationship due to Peter's threefold denial of Jesus on the night of Christ's arrest (see John, chapter 21). I interpret this episode as indicating that Self knows how to heal our parts, and stands ready to restore them and to empower them to rise to new positive roles.

We see a very similar pattern depicted with Thomas, in the famous episode commonly referred to as "Doubting Thomas," about which I have written extensively in *Myth and Trauma* and in *Star Myths of the Bible*. As with the restoration of Peter, the Thomas episode emphasizes the love and compassion of Self for the parts, and also the fact that the proper relationship of parts to Self is only achieved when the parts acknowledge and follow the lead of Self (similar, I would argue, to the proper role between players on a team and their coach).

Perhaps most remarkably, and in a lesson most clearly accessible to us if we are able to see the celestial foundations of the ancient myths, we see in the story of Perseus and Medusa a progression which dramatizes not only the heartbreaking process by which an innocent and beautiful young part is transformed by trauma into a lonely exile bearing a toxic curse, but which ends with Perseus marrying the beautiful Andromeda, almost as if Medusa is replaced by (or transformed into) Andromeda and restored from rape and exile to marriage and community.

As we have already seen, the arrangement of the constellations in the heavens leave absolutely no doubt that Medusa is associated with the constellation Andromeda: the constellation Pegasus can be seen to be emerging from the neck of Andromeda in the sky, just as the ancient myths tell us that Pegasus emerges from the neck of Medusa after Perseus cuts off her head.

Immediately afterwards, Perseus is flying back home and encounters Andromeda chained to a rock. Is it not interesting that the same constellation which down through the millennia has been called Andromeda (and which does, as H. A. Rey points out, have stars in its outline which could be envisioned as chains around its wrists, representing the chains binding the beautiful princess in the story) is the very same constellation which clearly plays the role of Medusa?

It is as though the entire story demonstrates the transformation of Medusa, guided by Athena, for our benefit and understanding, and application in this life.

Chapter Five

What would Ophiuchus do

In a sermon delivered on June 28th, 1891 by Baptist preacher Charles H. Spurgeon (1834 – 1892), entitled "The agreement of salvation by faith with walking in good works," Spurgeon elaborates on his view of how we put away unwelcome behavior and instead demonstrate "good works," becoming more "holy" in our lives, a view informed by his literalist reading of Biblical texts and his understanding of the person of Jesus as an external savior upon whom we are to believe in order to "be saved." In that sermon, Spurgeon declares:

> Our good works must flow from our union with Christ by virtue of our faith in him. We depend upon him to make us holy. We depend upon him to keep us holy. We overcome sin by the blood of the Lamb. We reach after holiness by the constraining love of Jesus. Love to Christ is the impelling cause of the putting away first one evil, and then another; and the energy enabling us to follow after one virtue, and then another. Love to Christ burns like a fire in the breast that has

conceived it; and, as it burns, it makes the heart to glow, and to become transformed to its own nature. You have seen a piece of iron put into the fire, all black or rusty, and in the fire it has become gradually red with heat; and, as it has reddened, it has thrown off the scales of rust, until it has looked itself to be a mass of fire. The effect of the love of God, shed abroad in the heart by the Holy Ghost, is to burn off the rust and scales of sin and depravity, and we become pure love to God through the force of the love of God, which takes possession of our being.[90]

Spurgeon was an immensely popular preacher during his lifetime, regularly packing the largest church building in England of its day to standing-room only capacity, with people lining up outside well in advance of the doors opening just to get a seat, and his sermons (transcribed as he delivered them by stenographers) remain popular today among literalist Christians who agree with his interpretations of the Bible. He can perhaps be considered one of the most winsome of apologists for a literalist reading of the ancient scriptures of the Bible, and one of the most articulate and most capable of putting a positive and attractive spin on doctrines derived from a literalist reading of those texts, and yet despite all his rhetorical and intellectual gifts, the position he defends in his sermons is fatally flawed by nature of the fact that the scriptures can be manifestly proven to be metaphorical rather than literal, and thus the more serious the attempt to rigorously force a literal interpretation upon them, the more convoluted and unnatural become the dogmas which the literalist is forced to adopt.

In this sermon, Spurgeon endeavors to defend the conventional doctrine, held as central across virtually all literalist Christian camps, that "faith in

Christ" — meaning acceptance and acknowledgement of the literal and historical life of a figure named Jesus, including all his works and especially his historical death on a physical cross as an atonement for the sins of those chosen to be saved, followed by his literal resurrection and ascension into heaven — is necessary to be "saved," meaning to be saved from punishment in eternal hell-fire after death.

This literalistic mis-interpretation can in and of itself be seen to be trauma-inducing, employing the threat of eternal damnation to induce acceptance of the historicity and literality of stories which are themselves esoteric and celestially metaphorical in nature, rather than literal and earthly. They are also exclusivist, demanding that men and women accept the literality and historicity of the Jesus stories in order to escape such eternal damnation, to the exclusion of, for instance, the stories of the life of the Buddha (whose birth-story was recorded well before the supposed historical period in which Jesus is said to have lived, and the details of which show such astonishing parallels to the gospel accounts of the birth of Jesus that we would be forced to believe that the gospel writers had copied the Buddha birth-accounts, if we did not know that the myths and scriptures and sacred stories of virtually every culture around the globe are based on celestial metaphor and are probably descended from some far more ancient common source).

I have previously shown, for example, that the story of the visit of the Magi described in the gospel according to Matthew cannot possibly be understood as literal and terrestrial history, following the arguments of another English-born preacher whose life predated that of Spurgeon by a generation and who went from being an enthusiastic evangelist for the literalist position to becoming one of the most insightful and articulate expositors of the evidence that the figures and stories of both the Old and New Testaments are based on the stars, the Reverend Robert Taylor (1784 – 1844), expelled from being a pastor of the Church of England for his views and even imprisoned multiple times for heresy. In my 2016 book *Star Myths of the Bible*, I show with maps and star-charts how the story of the "wise men from the east" (Matthew 2: 1) who follow "his star which they saw in the east" and which "went before them until it came and stood over where the young child was" (Matthew 2: 2 and Matthew 2: 9), cannot possibly be reconciled with a literal and terrestrial history, unless one maintains that the wise men somehow traveled from a position east of Jerusalem towards Asia and then continued following the star which they saw in the east until they had crossed the Pacific Ocean, landed somewhere in the Americas, crossed the Americas either by journeying across North America, Central America, or South America (or else going around Cape Horn between Tierra del Fuego and Antarctica), and then continued following the star seen in the east until they entered the Mediterranean through the Straits of Gibraltar and proceeded eastward through that region or across that sea until they came to Bethlehem.

I also show, still following the arguments laid out by Robert Taylor in his analysis of the visit of the Magi, how the text which makes no sense if we try to force it into being literal and historical, makes perfect sense if we understand that the gospel account is talking about the stars above, which do indeed rise in the east every night and proceed towards the west — a fact which also accounts for the line in the Matthew text which declares that these wise men later "departed into their own country another way" (Matthew 2: 12), by which we should understand that the stars which represent the wise men returned "to the east" by disappearing beneath the horizon in the west and then reappearing in the east on the next revolution of our planet.

There are many more examples of texts about Jesus which make it perfectly clear that the stories are based upon celestial metaphor — the exclamation attributed to John the Baptist upon seeing Jesus approaching the Jordan is another example, and that particular episode includes the telling statement by John the Baptist who says, "he must increase, but I must decrease" (John 3: 30), which perfectly describes the behavior of a constellation seen rising in the east from the perspective of a different constellation which is setting in the west.

Trying to take these stories literally, when they themselves manifestly demonstrate to us that they are celestial and metaphorical rather than literal, will thus end up creating knotty and insoluble logical problems for literalists, forcing them into ever more convoluted contortions of epistemology, and inevitably leading to severe distortions of the actual message contained in the stories. The core of the problem is that a literal interpretation, by definition, makes the stories about *external* characters (making Jesus and the twelve disciples, for instance, into historical persons and thus outside of us and external to us), when an interpretation which begins with the understanding that the characters are *metaphorical* leads to the realization that they are trying to show us something that pertains to *us* and that is in fact *internal* and esoteric.

Thus Spurgeon's arguments cited above, in which he tells his listeners that desirable behavior changes by which "sin and depravity" will fall away based on "love to Christ" burning in the breast of the individual (by which he means love of an external, historical Jesus in whose life and death on the cross the individual has believed and then continues to believe and look towards throughout his or her life), is dangerously flawed — and can very well end up leading to serious anguish and even despair in the life of the believer who accepts this description of the path towards "holiness."

As we have already seen, behaviors that Spurgeon would characterize as "sin and depravity" (such as, for example, use of alcohol to quench the pain of a triggered exile who carries a burden of shame or or guilt or heartbreak) are caused by parts who have taken on firefighter roles, and who are using those behaviors (whether compulsive drinking, compulsive shopping, compulsive sexual activity of some sort, compulsive eating, compulsive cutting of one's own body, or other actions intended to divert attention from the ancient trauma borne by the exiled part, such as explosions of rage or even drifting into distraction or off to sleep) to try to ensure the survival of the entire internal family. Looking to an external example or trying to "measure-up" to a set of external rules of piety, which Dr. Schwartz and IFS would characterize as a different category of defensive behavior typical of "manager" parts, can also help suppress the memory of the heartache or trauma but will also break down occasionally (those occasions, when the best efforts of the manager parts fail to prevent the triggering of the exile, being the usual signal to the firefighter parts to fly in and initiate their more drastic — and perhaps "depraved" — attempts to put out the blaze).

In the sermon cited above, Spurgeon continues on with his formula for overcoming depravity by imitating Jesus, referencing the autobiographical text *De Imitatione Christi* ("The Imitation of Christ") by Thomas à Kempis (1380 – 1471). Explicitly telling his listeners to try to imagine what the external historical figure of Jesus might do in any given situation, Spurgeon says:

> "The Imitation of Christ" is a wonderful book upon the
> subject, which every Christian should read. It has its faults,
> but its excellences are many. May we not only read the book
> but write it out anew in our own life and character, by seeking

in everything to be like to Jesus! It is a good thing to put up in your house the question, "What would Jesus do?" It answers nine out of ten of the difficulties of moral casuistry. When you do not know what to do, and the law seems not very explicit upon it — put it so: "What would Jesus do?"[91]

This passage articulates the approach of a great many literalist interpreters of the Bible, whether or not they are specifically Reformed Baptists as was Spurgeon in his day. Notice that he advises his listeners to actually post a sign or notice-board of some sort in their homes, bearing the words "What would Jesus do?" as a kind of touchstone to which they could look when in doubt of the way to act or decide. In more recent decades, a sign within the home being apparently not enough of a constant reminder, literalist Christians have taken to wearing mass-produced wristbands bearing the initials "WWJD" in order to remind themselves even more insistently to try to measure up to the external example of the supposedly literal and historical figure of Jesus.

Spurgeon even says explicitly that the right approach is "seeking in everything to be like to Jesus!" And there is no doubt that Spurgeon himself, as well as countless other followers of the literalist prescription, have heroically and valiantly expended tremendous energy in an effort to do just that, as often as they can remind themselves to do so. It is a distinctly "manager"-type approach to dealing with buried trauma and shame and grief and guilt and heartbreak, to try and live life by conforming to a set of external rules of piety and — when an explicit rule cannot be found in the "rulebook" of do's and don't's — to fall back upon an imitation of the behaviors dramatized by the figure of Jesus in the gospels. Note that Spurgeon actually expresses his advice in just such a manner: he says that this question of "What would Jesus do?" can be used as a kind of "last resort," when (as he says) "the law seems not very explicit upon it."

In other words, the literalistic approach to the scriptures of the Bible (as with literalistic approaches to other sets of ancient texts), veers by its very externalizing epistemological approach towards "trying to measure-up" to a set of external rules, and, when those rules fail to explicitly address some unforeseen situation, the literalist can solve the dilemma by imitating an admired external figure.

Whatever might be said about the benefits of such a prescription, it has a fatal flaw which the reader has no doubt already perceived: no amount of managerial behavior actually addresses the deep burden or burdens carried by the exiles of our internal family, and without actually dealing with those burdens, and healing and transforming those exiles, no amount of rule-following or pietistic behavior will ever "measure-up," leading to situations in which the mounting sense of guilt or shame or pain will (either slowly, or else suddenly) become unbearable, necessitating a sudden intervention from a firefighter, likely resulting in more shame and remorse and an even fiercer determination by the manager parts to try to live up to the impossible list of rules, or the impossible example of the chosen Christ-figure.

Indeed, there are some signs that Spurgeon himself suffered from depression and internal torment throughout his life, including evidence in the writings of his own wife about her observation of her husband's bouts of deep anguish and despair.

Think about the tacit message inherent in a formula which tells us that the road to holiness involves reference to an external rules and (when those rules fail to cover everything), imitation of an external supposedly literal perfect figure: you are not inherently worthy and valuable in-and-of-your-self, but must seek your worth through appeal to outside authority. Such a message leads to constant reference outwards, hoping for acceptance (either from other people, or from a projected external divinity, or both). Such a message leads to the opposite of facing life through expression of authentic Self. It is the very opposite of the message that each and every one of us has intrinsic internal and inalienable worth for who we are — and it will ultimately lead to neurosis. It is also false, because our worth and value as men and women is *not* dependent upon external appeal and the opinion and acceptance of others (whether those others are real or imagined).

But the good news is that, in common with the life-giving wisdom preserved in the ancient scriptures, myths, and sacred stories of cultures on every continent and island of our world, the scriptures of the Bible have at their heart the recovery of Self and the healing of trauma, and when understood as metaphor can be seen to dramatize this very subject, over and over and over again.

I would argue that those who gravitate to those scriptures of the Bible in search of healing for trauma are actually looking in the right place, for the stories of the Bible deal with that very subject as one of their most central concerns — but the tragic hijacking of those scriptures by the teachers of literalist doctrines built upon literalist interpretation has for the past sixteen centuries (at least) diverted those seekers into mostly unhelpful (and in at least some cases if not most cases, exceedingly harmful and traumatizing) mis-interpretations of their message. This is nowhere more evident than in the various forms of literalist Christianity arguing that the solution to the individual's most pressing issues involves acceptance of a literal and historical Jesus — in direct opposition to what those stories should be understood as teaching.

In fact, as argued by English poet, autodidact and early Egyptologist Gerald Massey (1828 – 1907), the author of most of the letters attributed to the writer calling himself "Paul" speaks of a "Christ within" who has nothing to do with a supposed historical or literal Jesus, and whose writings should actually be understood to be berating the idea of a literal Christ of flesh and blood.

In a lecture entitled "Paul the Gnostic Opponent of Peter, not a supporter of Historical Christianity," published among a series of ten bound lectures in London in 1900 and therefore originally delivered sometime before that, Massey argues that in the epistles attributed to Paul, we hear "two voices" uttering two distinctly different doctrines or teachings, doctrines "so fundamentally opposed as to be forever irreconcilable."[92]

These two conflicting voices, Massey argues, did not proceed from the same person, so opposite are they. One of them, Massey says, teaches what he calls a "spiritual Christ," that is to say, a "Christ within," which I would argue to be completely compatible with the concept of Self found within each one of us. The other, completely opposing position is represented by a voice presenting what Massey calls "the historic Jesus," by which he means the teaching of a literal, historical figure named Jesus — a proposition and a teaching which Massey argues to be diametrically opposed to the first position, and which he also refers to as the teaching of "Christ carnalised" (in other words, "made flesh").[93]

The two voices are so divergent, Massey argues, that one of them must have been falsely inserted into the other as part of a fraudulent attempt to co-opt the authority of the original writer — and Massey declares that the forgers must necessarily have been the proponents of a literalized or carnalized Jesus, because the esoteric understanding of a *Christ within* (or, as Massey often terms it, the Gnostic understanding) is much less obvious and much more likely to be opposed and rejected by the natural self-defense mechanisms which we have already examined than would be the simple recital of literal, historical facts which the "carnalizers" are trying to claim. Massey states:

> Now, it is quite certain that these Gnostic doctrines could not have been interpolated in Paul's writings by the founders of the Fleshly Faith. Therefore, it is the physical dogmas that have been foisted into the Epistles of Paul. I have never yet seen a sign in the works of Christian writers that they knew anything whatever of the real nature of these doctrinal mysteries. All alike are ignorant of the Tradition or Gnosis on which a true explanation depended. They assume the human history as the initial point of a new beginning, and ignore, or are ignorant of, that which lies beyond. When called upon to face the facts in broad daylight they themselves will be all in the dark, and will have to fight against them blindfold. But it is impossible to enter within range of understanding Paul's teaching until we do know something of the doctrines that were unfolded in the mysteries. It is impossible to comprehend the mystery of Paul's Christ without a fundamental knowledge of the Messianic mystery that has been from the Beginning. This was his mystery, which he would not make so much of if he had started with what are held to be plain historical gospel truths.[94]

In other words, Massey argues that Paul is articulating a mysterious and esoteric understanding, and one which was completely missed by the teachers of a carnal or "fleshly" Jesus, literalizers who clumsily inserted passages within some of the letters of Paul (and completely forged some others which are wrongly attributed to the same author) in order to try Paul into a support for their literalist project, although not very convincingly.

The writer calling himself Paul, as Massey points out, insists several times that he received his revelation regarding a *Christ within* directly from the divine, and not through any human source or scripture or teacher (in the very opening verse of each of the letters to the Galatians, Colossians, and Ephesians, for example). Says Massey, "He did not derive his facts from history, nor his gospel from the Apostles; he was neither taught by man nor book. He derived his Gospel from direct personal revelation of the Christ within."[95]

Those same letters angrily denounce and warn against the teaching of a fleshly Christ, for instance when the text of the letter to the Galatians asks, with evident exasperation: "Are ye so foolish? having begun in the spirit, are ye now made perfect by the flesh?" (Galatians 3: 3). And in the second letter to the Corinthians, he is equally disturbed, exclaiming, "Know ye not your own selves, how that Jesus Christ is within you?" (2 Corinthians 13: 5).

Literalizers might argue that this last verse contains the concluding phrase, "except ye be reprobates," but this counterargument can be parried by observing that Paul is here and elsewhere clearly arguing for an internal and spiritual Christ while berating those who later fall for those pushing stories of a fleshly and historical and external Jesus, and that thus the phrase "except ye be reprobates" may be understood as meaning "unless you too are reverting to a carnal understanding of what is, in fact, an esoteric and internal teaching that you are now abandoning."

Further support for the argument that it was the carnalizers who altered the originally esoteric letters, as opposed to the rather ridiculous other possibility that it was some esoteric advocate who tried to smuggle the teaching of a "Christ within" into what started out as essentially literalist teachings, comes from Massey's simple but devastating observation that it is the carnalizers who have controlled the texts and the doctrines and the established church hierarchies from the early centuries right down to this day.

Regarding these carnalizers or teachers of a literal and historical and external Jesus, Massey says of Paul:

> On comparing notes [with the literalistic proponents], he [Paul] found that they were preaching quite *another* gospel, and *another* Jesus. We know what their gospel was, because it has come down to us in the doctrines and dogmas of historic Christianity. It was the gospel of the literalisers of mythology; the gospel of the Christ made flesh to save mankind from an impossible fall; the gospel of salvation by the atoning blood of Christ; the gospel that would make a hell of this life, on purpose to win heaven hereafter; the gospel of flesh and physics, including the corporeal resurrection, and the immediate ending of the world; the gospel that has no other world except at the end of this. Theirs was that other gospel with its doctrines of delusion, against which Paul waged continual warfare. For *another Jesus, another Spirit*, and *another gospel*

were being preached by these pre-eminent apostles who were the opponents of Paul. He warns the Corinthians against those "pre-eminent apostles," whom he calls false prophets, deceitful workers, and ministers of Satan, who came among them to preach *another Jesus* whom he did not preach, and a different gospel from that which they had received from him.[96]

If we accept Massey's argument, and a careful reading of the entire lecture reveals abundant and compelling evidence to support the conclusions that Massey is arguing, then the entire literalist project can be shown to be not just in error from the beginning, but actually fraudulent practically from the outset. It is not simply a case of an "honest mistake," if the literalists actually tried to twist those epistles into supporting their positions by inserting fraudulent interpolations into the text.

As an aside, I agree with the major points which form the framework of Massey's argument in "Paul the Gnostic Opponent of Peter, not a supporter of Historical Christianity," although I do disagree with Massey's apparent assumption throughout the lecture that these carnalizers included the literal historical personage known as Peter. The Peter in the gospel stories can be confidently associated with the "hasty" and "headstrong" constellation Aquarius, as I have argued in *Star Myths of the Bible* and elsewhere, based in part on similar arguments put forth by Robert Taylor in lectures he gave during his lifetime, collected into two volumes published after his death entitled *The Devil's Pulpit* and *Astronomico-Theological Lectures* (both published in 1857).

Some of the arguments Taylor offers for the identification of Peter with Aquarius include the fact that Peter is traditionally associated with "holding the keys" to the kingdom of heaven, based upon the verse in Matthew 16: 19 in which Jesus says to Peter: "And I will give unto thee the keys to the kingdom of heaven: and whatsoever thou shalt bind on earth shall be bound in heaven: and whatsoever thou shalt loose on earth shall be loosed in heaven."

In a lecture delivered by Robert Taylor on 20 February, 1821 and collected into the *Devil's Pulpit*, Robert Taylor makes the brilliant and indisputable connection between Peter as "keeper of the keys" and the very important Roman god Janus, who was also depicted in ancient iconography as holding keys — and also as being accompanied by a cock or rooster, since Janus was the god of beginnings, including the beginning of the year but also of each day. Taylor notes that Janus as god of beginnings is the deity after whom the month of January is named, and that the sun passes through the zodiac constellation of Aquarius during that month — hence a strong reason for associating Peter with Aquarius as well.[97]

In the two images above, neither of which is from the actual ancient period but both of which incorporate symbology known to be associated with

Janus from extensive mentions in ancient texts, Janus is shown with his typical "two-faced" head, in which one face can be seen to look in the opposite direction from the other, and in both images he is shown holding a large key. In the first image, on the left as we face the page, which is from 1550, Janus also holds a grapevine, and Aquarius is nearby to the Great Square of Pegasus, which I have shown to be associated with a vineyard in a great many ancient myths and Bible stories, including the story of Balaam and the Ass (Numbers 23 and 24) and in the story of Noah after the Flood, who plants a vineyard and becomes drunk.

In the story of Noah, extensive evidence links Noah to Aquarius as well, which further supports the assertion that Peter is also connected to Aquarius, since Janus is connected to the grapevine (as is Noah, and Noah is Aquarius) and since Janus is associated with a large key (as is Peter).

In the second of the two images, on the right as we face them, which is from an engraving published in 1878 but also based on ancient precedents, Janus holds a key as in the first image, but this time instead of a vine, he carries a staff. While it is beyond doubt that figures associated with the constellation Ophiuchus often hold a spear or a staff in ancient myth, there are also many examples of figures associated with Aquarius holding a staff, due to the fact (I have argued) that the "forward leg" of the outline of Aquarius as shown below can be envisioned in some cases as a staff (and, in the story of Noah becoming drunk and then being uncovered and naked in front of his sons in the story of Shem, Ham and Japheth, this same forward leg can be envisioned as a certain portion of the male anatomy):

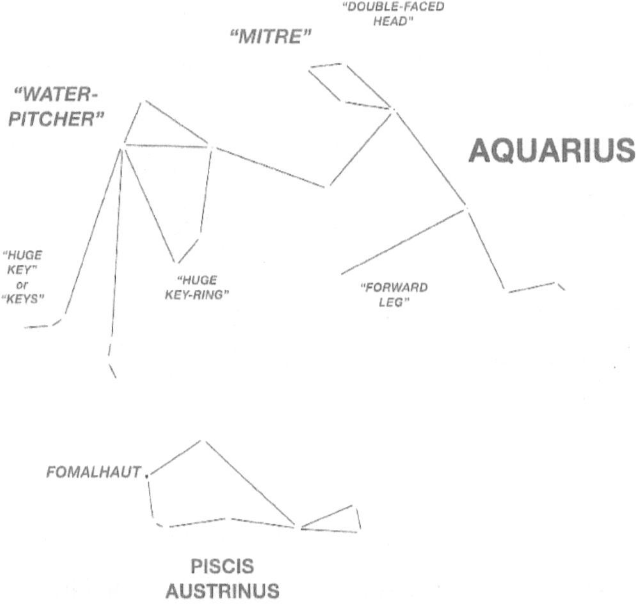

Note that in the above outline, I have added some of In my own interpretations of the constellation which I believe to be connected to the mythical interpretations of the identity of Peter and his connection to the god Janus. While I am indebted to Robert Taylor's arguments for making the connection between Peter and Janus, the constellational details above are my own analysis and not found in Taylor's lectures on Peter.

The oversized key carried by Janus, and associated as well with Peter, could well be a way of envisioning the portion of the constellation Aquarius which is usually envisioned as the "water-pitcher" or "water-jug" of the constellation, pouring out two streams of water. The stars themselves make two little "feet" at the bottom of these two streams of water coming down from the water-pitcher, each turning in a different direction. These could instead be envisioned either as two huge keys dangling from a great key-ring carried by Aquarius (the body of the pitcher being the key-ring and the two streams being two keys on the key-ring), with the two key "bits" pointing to either side. Note that Peter is usually depicted holding two keys (symbolizing the keys to heaven and earth, and the powers of binding and loosing, as mentioned in the text of Matthew 16: 19 cited above).

Note also that the head of the constellation Aquarius itself is formed by four stars in a tall "diamond" shape which very much resembles the bishop's mitre adopted by the hierarchies of the literalist church and associated with bishops including the Bishop of Rome (the Pope), who is specifically said to be given the authority first bestowed upon Peter in that verse about the keys found in Matthew 16: 19, thus providing yet another piece of celestial evidence from the constellation's outline to support the association of Peter and Aquarius.

Significantly, this diamond-shaped head of Aquarius enables us to envision the head as simultaneously looking in opposite directions — in other words, as if it has a face on both sides of the diamond, each looking in opposite directions and presenting us with a profile, as the god Janus with his two faces is traditionally depicted. This connection to the constellation itself helps to cement the identification of Janus with Aquarius as argued by Robert Taylor — and thus also supports the connection of Peter to Aquarius because both Peter and Janus are associated with keys.

In the outline of the constellation Aquarius, I have also labeled the outline of the constellation of Piscis Austrinus, the Southern Fish, which is found in the sky directly below Aquarius and beneath the "streams of water" that Aquarius is pouring down from the water-jug. The brightest star of this constellation, and by far its most noticeable feature, is the important star Fomalhaut, located at the tip of the front of the constellation, and thus known as the "Mouth of the Fish" (which is the meaning of the Arabic name Fomalhaut).

This aspect of the Southern Fish provides yet further evidence for associating Peter with Aquarius, seen in the story in which Jesus directs Peter to catch a fish in order to pay tribute money that was requested of Jesus and his disciples upon their arrival to Capernaum, recounted in Matthew chapter 17. In that episode, Jesus tells Peter: "go thou tothe sea, and cast an hook, and take up the fish that first cometh up; and when thou hast opened his mouth, thou shalt find a piece of money: that take, and give unto them for me and thee" (Matthew 17: 27). The coin in the mouth of the fish (described in the original Greek text as a *stater* which was a silver coin equal to two or four drachmas and to about one shekel) is obviously the bright star Fomalhaut, and the fact that in this story Jesus specifically tells Peter to cast in his hook and pull out the fish with the coin provides additional evidence to support our identification of Peter with Aquarius.

In my own research of the myths, I have often found the constellation Aquarius to be associated with running, due to the outline of the constellation itself, and therefore with both hastiness and impulsiveness, which are certainly characteristics associated with the figure of Peter in the gospel accounts. Note how the constellation, based on the actual arrangement of the stars in the sky, appears to be running at full speed: running so fast, in fact, that the running figure is practically falling forward (I have shown in *Star Myths of the World, Volume Two* that this aspect of Aquarius helps us identify figures who are described in the texts of the Iliad and the Odyssey as a "headlong runner" with Aquarius in virtually every instance in which that phrase is used).

Hence the mythological association of Aquarius with hastiness and with being "headstrong" and impulsive, which are obviously traits associated with certain of our parts, rather than with Self, whose characteristics as described by Dr. Richard Schwartz and IFS include calmness and clarity and other traits which contrast with the impulsiveness of the disciple Peter.

The larger point being argued here, of course, is the point we have been seeing supported by the evidence already examined in each of the chapters so far, which is the argument that the stories of the gospel (as with the other myths of the world) can be understood to dramatize for us a picture of our own internal landscape and its often-contentious internal family, in which the different parts have different characteristics and different strengths and weaknesses, and that Self is qualitatively different from the other parts in the same way that Jesus in the gospels is different from the disciples.

The characteristics of Self, including compassion and courage and clarity and curiosity and all the others which Dr. Schwartz identifies as being exhibited innately and universally, are all exhibited by Jesus in the stories. In the stories, we see that Jesus has the capability to heal even seemingly incurable afflictions, and that he shows compassion for those who are afflicted and the desire to heal them — even as Dr. Schwartz has invariably found that Self is capable of healing the various parts including exiles, even those carrying burdens so heavy and so painful that we might think they could never be transformed.

We might also note that in the stories, before healing someone, Jesus will frequently ask: "Do you want to be healed?" (for example, in the episode at the "sheep gate" of Bethesda described in John chapter 5, where in verse 6 we are told that Jesus asks a man "Wilt thou be made whole?"). This detail is also consistent with the experience of Dr. Schwartz based on interactions with thousands of patients, and interactions with their parts, and shows us that when we approach any part, we cannot force it to change — but Self can ask if that part wishes to be healed, and can with permission relieve its burden and make it whole.

Notice how different this understanding is from the prescription recommended by Charles Spurgeon which is a necessary outgrowth of centuries of reading the texts literally, and thus centuries of seeing Jesus as an external figure rather than as an esoteric dramatization of the power and characteristics of Self (power and characteristics already available to us, and not external to us). Instead of trying to imagine at every moment "what Jesus would do" and attempt to live up to that ideal (an ultimately impossible, futile, and even despair-inducing standard to achieve through the effort of even our most earnest and well-intentioned manager parts), the liberating message of the ancient myths is that we already have Self within us, and the more we can allow our various parts to "un-blend" from Self and to allow Self to take the lead (as Doubting Thomas finally does, when he acknowledges the lordship and primacy of Jesus in John 20: 28), the more we will exhibit those characteristics of Self which are already inside us.

The difference between the two understandings and approaches could not be more stark. We can sense why the ancient letters written by the esoteric practitioner calling himself "Paul" are so insistent on the point that *the Christ is in you*, and so dismayed to see his readers turning away to follow after "carnalizing" teachers who tell them instead that they must understand and accept and declare that Jesus is a flesh-and-blood figure.

Paul is aghast. He knows that carnalizing this inner truth into something or someone outside of us will only lead to the hopeless prescription that we find articulated quite openly and candidly in Spurgeon's sermon: follow *external* laws to know what to do in any given situation (instead of rea-soning for yourself), and if you encounter a situation which the law does not address explicitly enough for you ("when you do not know what to do, and the law seems not very explicit upon it," Spurgeon says), then make sure you have a sign hanging around your house, or a wristband hanging around your wrist, to remind you to ask yourself "What would Jesus do?" in that situation, thus giving you one final outside source to consult, just in case the list of laws doesn't address every single situation you might ever encounter.

In condemnation of this entire approach, Paul explodes: "Know ye not your own selves, how that Jesus Christ is within you?"

And this same argument can be applied to the literalistic and externalizing (or "carnalizing") of other mythical figures, especially those whose behaviors and characteristics clearly indicate that they are dramatizing Self for our better understanding.

For example, the figure of the Buddha can be shown to be based on the stars, as I have shown in the *Ancient World-Wide System* through extended discussion and numerous illustrative star-charts.

As briefly mentioned above, the birth-story of the Buddha has remarkable parallels to the birth-story of Jesus in the gospels, despite the fact that some of the oldest surviving Buddhist texts indicate the existence of Buddhism at least a hundred years prior to conventional "time of Jesus" and despite the fact that conventional dating of the life of the Buddha (the supposedly historical and literal person of the Buddha) puts his birth around 550 BC or BCE.

In the accounts of the birth of the Buddha-to-be, we learn that his mother conceives the child through a form of immaculate conception, without having sexual intercourse with a man but instead through a dream in which a white elephant enters her side. When the child is to be born, a host of overjoyed heavenly beings announce their happiness to a sage recluse named Asita, as described in the Pali Canon, the oldest set of texts in Buddhism.

There, in the Sutta Nipata of the Pali Canon, in the third section or chapter (entitled the Mahavagga, or "The Great Chapter"), the sage Asita tells his nephew Nalaka what happened on that momentous day: seeing heavenly devas of the Group of Thirty (the text says) rejoicing and cheering and waving banners, the seer asks them why they are so overjoyed.

The devas reply that the Boddhisatta (or "Buddha-to-be") has been born that day for the blessing of all the world, and declare that:

> "He, the highest of all beings, / The ultimate person, / a bull among men, foremost of all people, / will set turning the Wheel / in the grove named after the seers, / like a strong, roaring lion, the conqueror of beasts."[98]

Thus informed, Asita hastens to the place where the proud parents are holding their child, declares his blessing, and then breaks down in tears. The parents of the Buddha-to-be are very concerned upon seeing the great sage and seer Asita weeping just after declaring that their son is very special, and they ask Asita if he knows of some danger in the future for the young prince.

Asita replies,

> "I foresee for the prince no harm. / Nor will there be any danger for him. / This one isn't lowly: be assured. / This prince will touch the ultimate self-awakening. / He, seeing the utmost purity, / will set rolling the Wheel of Dhamma / through sympathy for the welfare of many. / His holy life will spread far and wide. / But as for me, my life here has no long remainder; / my death will take place before then. / I won't

get to hear the Dhamma of this one with the peerless role. /
That's why I'm stricken, afflicted, and pained."[99]

The parallels to the gospel stories about another supposedly historical birth could not be more plain. In both accounts, the ancient texts describe a spiritual or divine conception in the body of a mortal (but exceedingly virtuous) woman: in the case of Mary through the Holy Spirit as announced by the Angel Gabriel, and in the case of Maya mother of the Buddha-to-be through a dream in which she sees an elephant enter her right side, after which she awakens and knows she is now miraculously with child.

In both cases, a heavenly host announces their elation at the birth of the special child (devas or male celestial beings in the story of the birth of Buddha, and angels in the gospel accounts of the birth of Jesus), and in both cases there is the story of an old sage or holy man who visits the parents and declares to them that he will not live to see the wonders this child will bring, but that he can now depart in peace having seen the child's arrival.

The parallel story in the gospels is found in the book of Luke, in which we are told in chapter 2:

> And behold, there was a man in Jerusalem, whose name was Simeon; and the same man was just and devout, waiting for the consolation of Israel: and the Holy Ghost was upon him. And it was revealed unto him by the Holy Ghost, that he should not see death, before he had seen the Lord's Christ. And he came by the spirit into the temple: and when the

parents brought in the child Jesus, to do for him after the custom of the law, then he took him up in his arms, and blessed God, and said, Lord, now lettest thou thy servant depart in peace, according to thy word: For mine eyes have seen thy salvation, which thou prepared before the face of all people; a light to lighten the Gentiles, and the glory of thy people Israel. And Joseph and his mother marveled at those things which were spoken of him. And Simeon blessed them, and said unto Mary his mother, Behold, this child is set for the fall and rising again of many in Israel; and for a sign which shall be spoken against. Luke 2: 25 – 34.

In both stories, we see an old holy man who pronounces a blessing on the baby in the presence of the parents, and are told that the parents marvel at the arrival of this sage figure. Also in both stories, the old holy man declares that he shall not live to see the illustrious life of the baby. The parallels are extraordinary and point to either deliberate copying or descent from a common, more ancient tradition.

Even more striking is the fact that in the story of Asita, the old sage tells the astonished parents that this child shall "set rolling the Wheel of Dhamma" (or *Dharma*). In the Luke text, Simeon tells the parents of baby Jesus that "this child is set for the fall and rising again of many in Israel" (Luke 2: 34).

When we understand that the turning Wheel in the Buddha story refers to the great wheels of the heavens, and specifically the circle of the zodiac (note the reference to both a Lion and a Bull when the devas declare to Asita that the child shall be the one to set the Wheel turning), then we can see that this turning wheel in the heavens is also found in the Simeon text, where the sage old man says that the child will cause the *fall* and the *rising again* of many in Israel.

Approached with the understanding that the stories are based upon celestial metaphor, it is easy to see that the falling and rising of "many in Israel" refers to the turning of the same wheel of the zodiac that is declared in the Buddha story. We have already seen, in our discussion of the brothers of Joseph, that the children of Jacob (who is re-named Israel) are each associated with a constellation in the zodiac, a connection that is made explicit in Genesis 49, where the sons of Jacob (Israel) are listed and compared to "a lion's whelp" or an archer whose "bow abode in strength," and other descriptions which can be seen to point to specific zodiac signs.

Indeed, in the Simeon passage, the child himself is declared to be destined to be "a sign which shall be spoken against" (Luke 2: 34). Based on the analysis already set out in the previous chapters as well as this one, we can readily deduce that this text is suggesting that the Christ will be associated with the constellation Ophiuchus, that sign which is set apart from the other signs of the zodiac and which is in fact excluded from the zodiac, teaching us that in our own internal family the Self is different from the parts, and will even be denied and "spoken against" by the other parts (just as the story of Peter vigorously denying that he knows Jesus dramatizes for our understanding).

Abundant evidence points to the conclusion that the figure of the Buddha is also associated with the constellation Ophiuchus, including the famous episode of meditating beneath the Bodhi Tree (the "Tree of Awakening," traditionally understood to be a fig tree), which as I have shown in *Ancient World-Wide System* can be understood as a myth built upon the relative locations of Ophiuchus (the Buddha) and the constellation Hercules (the tree, when Hercules is envisioned in "whirling" form, discussed in the previous chapter in our examination of the olive tree sacred to the goddess Athena).

In the image above, we see a carved relief showing the Buddha under the sacred fig tree, dating back to around the first through third centuries AD (or CE). The star-chart shows Ophiuchus and the outlines of the "whirling form" of the constellation Hercules are depicted in order to show how Ophiuchus can be envisioned as sitting under the tree (note that in the Bible, there are other figures who are described as sitting under a fig tree, notably the disciple Nathanael in the gospel according to John, chapter 1).

In the ancient depiction of the Buddha, the artist has also added the powerful-looking figure of a man with a full beard, holding a mighty mace over his head, seen to the right of the seated Buddha as we look at the sculpture here. This figure is known as Vajrapani, because the great mace he is brandishing is the Vajra, or "thunderbolt weapon" of the ancient Sanskrit texts. We can easily see the correspondence between Vajrapani and the constellation Hercules (looking at the ancient sculpture, if we were not aware of the identity of a figure named Vajrapani, we would immediately guess that the figure looming behind the Buddha in the sculpture *is* a depiction of the mythical hero Hercules).

This inclusion of a Hercules-figure behind and above the serene figure of the Buddha should be enough to confirm that the Buddha is an Ophiuchus-related figure in ancient myth, but the sculptor has here added yet another confirmatory detail, in the form of an egg-shaped object in the upraised hand of the seated Buddha. This feature clearly corresponds to the "serpent's head" feature on one side of the constellation Ophiuchus (those who might resist this assertion should examine the many other examples of a similar "egg-shaped" object in an upraised hand, shown in *Ancient World-Wide System*, which confirm this assiociation beyond a shadow of a doubt).

The sculpture obviously shows the egg-shaped object in the hand on the left side of the body of the Buddha as we face the sculpture (the right hand), which is reversed from what we see in the star-chart (where the serpent's head of Ophiuchus is on the right side as we face the page, which is the west side of the constellation), but it is not uncommon for artists to sometimes exercise artistic license when depicting sacred scenes and figures from myth, and to reverse their subjects from what we see in the heavens, although the celestial correspondences are still unmistakable.

The point here is that the stories of the Buddha, like the stories of the Christ, should be understood to be illustrative of the properties of Self, rather than literal descriptions of the lives and adventures of historical persons. There are numerous Buddhist temples and holy sites which claim to have fig trees directly descended from the actual Bodhi Tree under which a historical Buddha sat (the oldest of these "direct descendent" trees is thought to have been planted as early as 250 BC, showing that the supposed time of the life of a literal and historical Buddha is centuries before the supposed time of the life of a literal and historical Jesus), but I would argue that the evidence is overwhelming for concluding that the stories of the Buddha, like the stories of Jesus, are celestial metaphor — and that the Bodhi Tree in the stories can still be seen to this day, shining in the heavens, rather than being a literal tree on earth.

Some will object that seeing the celestial foundations of these stories some-how "takes away" from our "devotion to" the Buddha or to the figure of Jesus — but to such an objection, we have to ask: "Why?" and "Really?" The very opposite could actually be argued: mis-placed devotion to an external and "carnal" Jesus or external and historical Buddha actually cause us to miss the meaning of the ancient myths, if the purpose of those myths is to enable us to grasp the fact that we already have access to our own Self, who inherently possesses all the positive traits dramatized in the stories about Jesus and Buddha.

In fact, as already argued (and as most of us will readily admit from our own experience, if we have lived this incarnate life for enough years), the attempt to "live up to" the example of a Jesus or a Buddha — if they are external figures — will ultimately be futile and lead to frustration and possibly despair.

However, if we understand that these stories are meant to point us to the reality of Self (and remember that, if we have suffered trauma and have become alienated from Self, then we have powerful defense mechanisms which can act to resist and reject the very existence of our authentic Self, whom we have buried away), and if we understand that as we allow the parts to "un-blend" from Self and even to acknowledge and to trust Self, and look to Self for leadership, then we will begin *organically* to exhibit those very characteristics of Self which are so elusive and so difficult to "imitate" when we are "trying" (through our parts) to ask ourselves "What would Jesus do?" or "What would Buddha do?" or to live up to some list of laws or other external code.

I would argue that all the various myth-systems and ancient philosophies of the world actually point us towards a fairly uniform and universal set of principles, which amount to some variation on the advice given over and over in various forms and through various metaphors by the divine Krishna (another higher Self figure who can be shown to correspond to the constellation Ophiuchus, as I have shown in *Ancient World-Wide System*) to the hero Arjuna: *Do what is right, without attachment.*

In late 1971 at a hill called Mawangdui in Changsha, the capital of Hunan province in China, workers from a city hospital were digging a deep hole into the side of the hill when they noticed the matches they used to light their cigarettes during a break were sparking eerie blue flames — frightening them to the point that they reported it to the authorities, who realized that gasses being emitted from inside the mound were the cause. An archaeological expedition, augmented by volunteers from local schools, uncovered in early 1972 three tombs sealed in the years 186 BC to 168 BC, one of them undisturbed and containing one of the best-preserved mummies ever found, and in the third tomb (believed to be either the son of the noble couple buried in the first two tombs, or perhaps the brother of the woman whose tomb was previously undisturbed) contained a number of precious astronomical texts and two copies inscribed on silk of the Tao Te Ching (or Dao De Jing), the earliest known surviving copies of that ancient classic that has ever been found, predating by more than a hundred years any previously-known copies of the Tao.

I have previously discussed clear celestial aspects of the Tao Te Ching (in *Ancient World-Wide System*), showing the initially-suprising evidence that it too has clear celestial components, including the well-known story of its legendary author Lao Tzu riding *into the west* on the back of an impressively-horned *bull* or water buffalo. In fact, a central theme throughout the text of the Tao, introduced in what has traditionally been arranged as the second of the chapters, is that the "multitude of things" arise from out of the nameless ineffable and then after a time disappear back into the undifferentiated again.

This pattern of everything arising out of the Tao and then dissolving and disappearing again can be compared to the turning of a wheel — and in fact the metaphors evoked in what is traditionally arranged as the eleventh chapter of the text of the Tao specifically evokes a turning wheel, and indeed one with "thirty spokes." Recall that in the story of Asita, the rejoicing devas who announced the birth of the Buddha-to-be were members of the "Group of Thirty" and that they specifically foretold that the Buddha would be the one who sets the great Wheel turning. As we saw, the turning of the great wheel is also indirectly referenced by the old sage Simeon at the birth of the Christ, specifically referencing the rising and falling of "many in Israel" — which I argue with very solid supporting evidence to be related to the turning of the specific wheel of the zodiac (the twelve signs of which correspond to the twelve children of Jacob-Israel, as well as to the twelve "tribes" or groups of stars who make up the zodiac constellations).

Note that if we divide any circle of 360 degrees into twelve equal sections, each section will have 30 degrees — and that we have a clear reference to the number thirty in both the vision of Asita and in Chapter 11 of the Tao Te Ching. The turning of the great wheel thus has metaphorical references to the turning of the great circle of the zodiac, which we have explored in this book as being representative of the various parts or personalities found in each of our internal families (with some of us receiving at birth more of the characteristics associated with this or that sign, and others of us receiving more of the characteristics associated with these or those other signs, in our own individual "recipe" that makes up our unique mix of gifts and traits and energies).

The image of the Buddha being the one who will turn this great wheel, or of the Christ child who will cause the falling and rising of "many in Israel," can thus be interpreted as teaching us that the divine Self, who is within each of us and who is among all of our other parts while yet being different from them, is the one who has primacy over the wheel and who is in some way its master — setting it to turning while yet being calm and clear and unattached or unaffected by the rising and falling, the manifesting and disappearing, the "ups and downs" that are part of every life.

In the text of the Tao describing the wheel, it is the "emptiness" that is made up of the space within the wheel that makes it useful, like the empty space within a clay pot and not the pot itself.

The principle of action (setting turning) while being in some way detached or unaffected is described in the Tao Te Ching as the famous ideal of *wu wei* meaning "non" or "empty" or "null" action or work. It is articulated with those very words many times within the text of the Tao, including in the second chapter as traditionally arranged, in the fourth stanza, where we are told words to the effect: "Therefore the master handles affairs with *wu wei* — effortless action without action."

In his 1990 translation of the Mawangdui texts of the Tao Te Ching, Professor Victor H. Mair discusses the concept of *wu wei* in an important and illuminating Afterword to the text. He writes:

If *Tao* and *te* are the most significant static or nounal concepts in the *Tao Te Ching*, *wu-wei* is certainly the most important dynamic or verbal notion set forth in the classic. Of all the Old Master's ideas, it is also the most difficult to grasp. *Wu-wei* does not imply absence of action. Rather, it indicates spontaneity and noninterference; that is, letting things follow their own natural course. For the ruler, this implies reliance on capable officials and the avoidance of an authoritarian posture. For the individual, it means accomplishing what is necessary without ulterior motive. Some commentators have explained *wu-wei* as connoting "non purposive" or "nonassertive" action.[100]

Professor Mair then elaborates further on this principle of non purposive action and notes strong parallels to the central theme of the Bhagavad Gita of ancient India, in which the Lord Krishna articulates very much the same concept to the wavering and uncertain hero Arjuna, prior to the great cataclysmic battle of Kurukshetra:

The chief lesson Krishna has to offer Arjuna is that altruistic or disinterested action (*niskama karma*) leads to realization of Brahma. That is to say, one should act without regard or desire for the fruits (*phala*) of one's action. This idea is repeated over and over again in countless different formulations. These passages are of great importance for understanding the enigmatic concept of "nonaction" that is so prominent in the *Tao Te Ching*. "The person of superior integrity takes no action," says the Old Master, "nor has he a purpose for acting." We are told straightaway to "act through nonaction" and that "through nonaction, no action is left undone." In spite of the fact that this idea appears a dozen times and is obviously central to the Old Master's teachings, we can only vaguely surmise from the *Tao Te Ching* the specific implications of *wu-wei* (nonaction).

However, when we read the *Bhagavad Gita*, we discover an exceedingly elaborate analysis of the nature and purpose of nonaction. The ideal of action without attachment is conveyed in many guises throughout the *Bhagavad Gita*, for example, *akrta* (nonaction), *akarma* (inaction), *naiskarmya* (freedom from action or actionlessness), *karmanam anarambhan* (noncommencement of action), and so forth. Krishna refers to himself as the "eternal nondoer" and states that the Yogin should think, "I do not do anything." He declares that he "sits indifferently unattached by these actions." Elsewhere he condemns sitting and remembering. All of this reminds us of the "sitting and forgetting" advocated by the Taoists that later developed into a type of meditative practice.[101]

We could note that the ancient stoic philosophers also aspired towards a similar ideal, which they described as freedom in harmony with divine all-pervasive reason, unclouded by the distracting and misleading "passions" generated by mistaken beliefs which diverge from that reason. It is well attested by the surviving writings of the early stoics, who flourished around 300 BC and in the centuries following, that their philosophy also described a world which cyclically unfolds from undifferentiated divine fire, and which periodically returns again to fire, only to unfold again, and again, much like the unfolding from and disappearing back into the Tao described in the Tao Te Ching, or the turning of the great Wheel of Dharma described in the ancient Buddhist texts and implied in the prophecy of Simeon found in the gospel according to Luke.

Once again, it is worth emphasizing the understanding of the interplay of parts and Self we have been exploring in this volume can shed positive light on this ideal of right action without attachment, without passions, being articulated across so many of the ancient traditions. It is an ideal that we know to be so elusive, so rare, and (if we have ourselves tried to pursue it) so impossible to achieve through even the very best efforts of our managerial parts.

But the solution is found in the understanding that Self intrinsically and inherently displays this very characteristic of *wu wei* action, when "unblended" from the well-meaning but often-mistaken "passions" of the various parts. Self, as we have seen, has clarity: Self knows how to act, knows what is needed, knows what to do and has the courage and confidence to do it. When we encounter "passions" that are uncharacteristic of Self, as Dr. Schwartz displays in his conversation with the woman suffering from anorexia who relays first an angry voice, then a confused voice, and then a tired voice (described in Chapter Two), we know that these are from parts: well intentioned and important parts of who we are, with important roles to play, but incapable of the same caliber of clarity, calm, and courageous action which Self unerringly displays, when we allow Self to come forth.

I would suggest that the remarkable parallels we have been exploring between the descriptions of the birth of the Buddha and of the birth of
the Christ, and the wheel imagery which they both share with the Tao
Te Ching and its articulation of the endless cyclical unfolding from and
disappearing back into the undifferentiated ineffable Tao, can be seen as
powerful confirmation of an ancient system which points us towards an
understanding of Self and parts using the metaphor of the turning wheel
of the zodiac (with all of the various zodiac constellations dramatizing
our various parts), with Ophiuchus as the sublime Self who sits above
all the others and who is yet compassionate and caring and ever-ready to
heal our parts and unburden them, and bring them into harmony while
allowing them to play the role for which they were designed and which
they themselves desire to play, the way a master conductor can harmonize
all the players of the symphony, or the way a wise and experienced coach can
bring out the best gifts of each member of a team and help them to all work
together to achieve what they might have previously thought impossible.

Indeed, there is yet one more remarkable correspondence between the
seemingly-disparate ancient texts describing the birth of the Buddha, the
birth of the Christ, and the story of the Tao Te Ching, and this remarkable
correspondence is only perceptible when we understand that the name of
the "Old Master" who supposedly dictated the ancient words of the Tao
before riding away into the west on a bull or buffalo, Lao Tzu or Laozi, is
composed of two Chinese characters which mean "Old Man" and "Child"!

As I have explained at some length in *Ancient World-Wide System*, this
name itself very much suggests the great wheel of the year! We can perhaps
best perceive this fact when we consider the popular symbology, still very
much used in the west around the time of "New Year's Day," of the handoff
between "Old Father Time" and "Baby New Year." The two allegorical

symbols are very much seen as being tied together or connected to one another: the "old man" with long beard representing the end of the past year must give way to the cherubic little baby, representing the potential of the new year that is just beginning. In many popular representations, these two are depicted as two different versions of the same "Father Time" figure we discussed in Chapter Three, associated with Kronos and Saturn and carrying a great scythe (associated with a Golden Age and clearly patterned upon the pivotal constellation of Ophiuchus in the night sky).

Thus, the very name of Lao Tzu which tradition associates with the giving of the wisdom in the Tao Te Ching evokes the great turning circle of the cycles of time, and the theme of the disappearing of the old only to be replaced again by the unfolding of the new, described in the text of the Tao itself and compared at one point explicitly to a wheel.

And, as we have already seen, we find the very same remarkable imagery dramatized in the stories of the birth of the Buddha and the birth of the Christ, where we see depicted for us an old man blessing the promised child, rejoicing over the baby's arrival, and then declaring to the parents that he himself (the old man) will now retreat from the stage and disappear, happy in the fact that he has seen the one who turns the wheel.

Chapter Six

Concluding Thoughts

And so we conclude where we began, with the understanding that the gods spoken of in the ancient texts are in very real sense within us already, and that this understanding (and its accompanying realization that we are a multiplicity in our internal family, rather than a "mono-mind" as Dr. Schwartz calls it) frees us from the errors and frustrations inherent in the prescription given by Charles Spurgeon and the literalists, who see unwelcome behaviors and "depravities" as accretions that we can "burn away" like rust flaking off of a lump of metal which is thrown into a fire, as if they are externalities to be shed.

We have seen abundant evidence of a system which spans multiple ancient systems which are thought to be separate and distinct from one another but which clearly employ celestial metaphor involving the turning wheel of the zodiac and the (often suppressed and excluded or "hidden" and "forgotten") thirteenth constellation of Ophiuchus, which can with ample justification be understood to be dramatizing a picture and an understanding of our own internal landscape consisting of various distinct parts, each important and each with important gifts and resources to contribute, but also prone to internal squabbles and discord, to suppression and exclusion of parts carrying our most toxic burdens and most painful heartbreaks, and to denial of our own authentic and divine higher Self, in whom they lose faith due to childhood trauma and attachment injury, despite the fact that Self is the one who can actually heal those burdens and injuries and restore harmony and balance to the whole family.

The ancient wisdom bequeathed to all the families of the nations of the world incorporate and dramatize a profound understanding of our internal landscape and the dynamics of our various inner personalities — as well as a beautiful vision of our transcendent and indestructible Self. And yet this amazing wisdom has been eclipsed by centuries of literalistic — and primarily monotheistic — mis-interpretation of the ancient stories, along with an aggressive proselytizing campaign of spreading literalistic monotheism to all corners of the globe, deliberately stamping out and destroying their traditional received wisdom in the process.

This aggressive campaign of world-conquest and empire-building fueled by literalism not only inflicted (and continues to inflict) physical violence and trauma upon its victims in the course of its expansionary project, but also internal and psychological trauma, including threat of eternal damnation and hellfire as punishment for unwelcome behaviors which we have seen can be best understood as roles taken up by our different parts in an attempt to hold the system together and to suppress deep psychological wounds and burdens. The prescription offered as the path to changing unwanted behaviors and "depravities" through attempted obedience to external sets of rules or laws, as expressed for example in the sections of Spurgeon's nineteenth-century sermon, or the suggested reminder to constantly ask "What would Jesus do?" can only lead to eventual frustration and despair — as well as additional anguish if the fear of eventual eternal damnation in a literal hell is also accepted as valid.

As we might expect, the threat of literal hell-fire be shown to be based on celestial metaphor, thus indicating that the texts are not describing what the literalists think they are describing: in other words, not a literal "hell" at all. The references to "the worm" mentioned in various texts throughout the Bible, including those texts in the gospels in which Jesus describes hell as the place where "their worm does not die, and the fire is not quenched" (such as in Mark chapter 9), can be confidently shown to be referring to the long and sinuous constellation Scorpio in the heavens ("the worm" which does not die), and to the "fire" of the column of the Milky Way (Scorpio is located at the part of the Milky Way where the river of stars is brightest and widest, and indeed the constellation Scorpio itself is half-way within that bright and wide part of the Galaxy band).

The ancient myths use the "lower half" of the zodiac wheel, when days are shorter than nights (which, for the northern hemisphere, means the days between the fall equinox, heading down to the winter solstice, and back up through the spring equinox) to represent *this incarnate life*, when we are "down here" in a body — and because Scorpio is on the way down towards the very lowest portion of this "lower half" of the zodiac, when the sun's journey is taking it towards its lowest arc of the year, in winter, we can conclude that this reference to a hell where the worm does not turn indicates that hell actually refers more to this incarnate life than to some imagined afterworld.

Thus the gospels are not about somehow escaping a literal hell at all, I would argue, but rather have as a central theme the recovery of Self, as we have been discussing — with the figure of Jesus portraying for us all the characteristic aspects of Self (as with other Self figures, almost always associated with Ophiuchus, in the other ancient myths of the world), not in order for us to try to somehow "imitate" these or "live up" to them by following an example, but rather by getting to know our different parts and their burdens, approaching them with compassion and respect and honoring their individuality and their efforts to try to protect us and help us succeed, and ultimately to ask them to relax and trust Self to arise, knowing that Self can and will step up and lead when we allow that to happen.

For sixteen or more centuries, literalist Christianity and other forms of literalistic monotheism imposed a mindset contrary to the pluralistic vision that is actually taught in the ancient myths and sacred stories (including in the stories of the Bible, if understood in a metaphorical and esoteric sense, instead of in a literalistic sense), but it is safe to say that during the nineteenth century and especially the twentieth century, the influence of literalistic interpretations diminished sharply (Charles Spurgeon, in fact, was active and outspoken in trying to combat the various assaults on the literalistic doctrines throughout his lifetime).

However, the relaxation of the grip of literalistic monotheism did not automatically lead to any kind of return to a more holistic understanding of our internal landscape and the multiplicity of our internal family — on the contrary, any gaps left by the retreat of literalism and its denial of the ancient gods and ancient wisdom were promptly filled by the onrush of a new kind of secular faith, the modernistic and aggressive "materialism" which denies the existence of anything beyond the strictly material realm and which certainly never teaches the existence of an innate and universal and indestructible Self, and certainly of any claim that through Self we have access to the divine and to divine inspiration and to insights that are difficult or even impossible to explain within a strictly materialistic paradigm.

Today, we live in a world in which these two different approaches still vie with one another, the two broad approaches (belief in one of the various literalistic systems, or a hard materialism which is presented as more "scientific" and empirically valid) existing together in a kind of uneasy truce, with some instances of increased polarization and hostility.

This situation, in which two different broad categories of world-view oppose one another in uneasy polarization but in which both of them basically deny and obscure the ancient understanding of "multiple parts plus indestructible and divine Self" actually very much resembles the dynamic we described earlier in which two opposing parts (often a manager and a firefighter, but other combinations are also possible, including two managers pursuing different strategies, or two firefighters who resort to different extreme tactics when trying to douse an internal flare-up) operate in a "polarized triangle" in order to suppress ancient heartbreak and trauma from the individual's past.

But the truth cannot remain suppressed forever: truth has a way of rising to the surface, no matter how vigorously it is pushed down by those who want to ignore or deny it.

The ancient gods given to humanity in the myths and sacred stories are not just the gods of our ancient collective past — if the gods are in some sense within us (and we have seen abundant evidence to conclude that they act through and in men and women in a very real sense, and that the ancient myths and traditions of the world teach that this understanding is true), then they are also the "gods of ancient you." Our own deep traumas and injuries, perhaps buried deeply or even completely ignored or forgotten by our conscious mind and by those parts who would prefer to act out their roles in denial of their own early life history, continue to echo down the corridors of the years and impact the behavior of all the different members of our internal family.

I would suggest that we can benefit not only from the ancient understanding preserved in the ancient stories, and from studying them for ways in which they can help us to gain insights about dealing with our own internal family, but that we might also profit from incorporating some of the lessons our ancestors pass down to us about dealing with the gods.

One very consistent pattern which we find in myth and sacred story around the world is the power of *verse* and metered language — as well as of music, which of course is inherently metered and rhythmic — when it comes to invoking or even describing the gods.

Around the world, the knowledge of the gods is preserved in the form of poetry and verse. Poetry differs from prose not primarily by rhyming (although poetry often does rhyme as well) but rather because poetry is *metered* prose: poetry observes deliberate rhythmic patterns in order to produce an effect which is different from the effect of prose (prose being un-metered).

From the Vedas of ancient India to the lines of the Gilgamesh poem, and from the Iliad and the Odyssey and the Theogony to the utterances of the Pyramid Texts of ancient Egypt, and from the Poetic Edda of Norse mythology to the songs of Maui among the cultures of the Pacific, and so on around the world, language spoken either *to* the gods or *about* the gods is almost universally preserved for us in verse or metered language, whether passed down in oral tradition or in written scripture.

Why might this be?

Well, it might be that metered language has an effect upon the gods them-selves, but it is certain that metered language has an effect *on us* — and as we have seen throughout this examination, the ancient wisdom teaches that the gods are in some way present in us. In fact, throughout this book we have seen that it would not be wrong on misguided to see each of our various parts as embodying some of the different characteristics of the various gods and goddesses described in the ancient traditions of the world.

In his introduction to the 2013 edition of his translation of the Orphic Hymns, Professor Apostolos N. Athanassakis discusses the power of verse and of repetition and of piled-up epithets describing the gods, exemplified not only in the Orphic Hymns but in other sacred traditions around the world. After mentioning "Indic, Iranian, and Muslim cult music" which "use song as a bridge by which to unite heaven and earth," and after show-ing remarkable parallels between the long lists of descriptive sea-related names of the various daughters of Nereus (the Nereids) and the equally long list of descriptive sea-related names given to the Virgin Mary in certain Christian traditions, and then noting that the Whirling Dervishes of the Mevlevi order incorporate the "emotionally powerful, indeed ecstatic and repetitive, invocation of Allah" in the recitation of Allah's ninety-nine names, among other examples Professor Athanassakis says:

> If we call all this a chain of similar religious phenomena, even
> a coincidental one, we may come closer to understanding the
> power of clustering epithets for the creation of an emotional
> and physical crescendo that might raise our human spirit and
> help us approach the divine. [. . .]

Clearly, elevation of mood and the powerful affirmation of a meaningful and bonding presence are elements that run through the recitation of mighty words and sacred sounds flowing into the eager ears and souls of the faithful. Even the puns serve this purpose. Names chanted or better yet sung or even simply recited in a particular sacred tone have power. Each epithet reverberates into the mind of the celebrant and spins out its own plot and its own action. As one epithet follows another, chains of meaning and sound acquire a power that may exceed that of a highly structured narrative. One name is one thing. Two names are more than two things. The Orphic Hymns are beautiful poetry of another kind, a transcendental kind, which must be understood in the context of its own conventions.[102]

The Orphic Hymns (as discussed in that same introduction) may date from any number of possible centuries — the authors of that introduction lean towards dating them to a period of Orphic revival during the Roman Empire's Severan Dynasty, late second and early third centuries CE, but likely drawing on centuries-long Orphic traditions and formulas — but they are certainly ancient, and preserve a powerful ancient technique for invoking the various gods. Other ancient material could of course be used instead, but if we wish to invoke Athena or Artemis, Apollo or Ares, Poseidon or Aphrodite, Hephaestus or Eros, Hekate or Hermes, Hera, Zeus, or Dionysus, or one of many other gods and powers to whom we find hymns within the received Orphic texts, the translation by Apostolos N. Athanassakis and Benjamin Wolkow is a tremendous resource to employ.

Most of the hymns come down to us with a suggested incense to light during the invocation, and in the introduction from the translators we find the suggestion to readers that they "raise their voices as they read to a pleasant and imposing pitch as well as a clear and rhythmically punctuated vocalization of the lines. The tone of voice should strive to approximate dignified chant."[103]

The fact that the Orphic Hymns all follow a general pattern of invoking the specific divinity, listing and praising their various attributes and epithets, and then asking for benevolence and good outcome from the deity who is being invoked, can be instructive to us in our own conversation with our own parts, our own internal carriers of the different aspects of the multiple gods and goddesses of humanity's received traditions.

We should always deal with our parts with respect and reverence, and request that they act in a way that is gracious and beneficial to us, with the expectation that when we thus invoke them, *they will*.

Note that in the ancient Vedic traditions, mantras are similarly used to invoke the deities. We have already seen the example of Dhruva, who in the Puranas is given a mantra to learn which he recites over and over until the god Vishnu appears to him. The ancient mantras, including the specific mantra traditionally understood to be the one used by Dhruva in the story — the *Dvadasakshari*, or "Twelve Syllable" Mantra: *Om Namo Bhagavate Vasudevaya* — are still recited to this day and can be found in many places and learned for the same purpose.

The Sanskrit mantras are understood to be effective even if one does not speak or understand Sanskrit: it is the rhythm and the meter and the combination of vowels and consonants and specific sounds themselves which invokes the power.

From this understanding we can surmise that, in addition to chanting and song and metered language, other forms of rhythmic sound can also be valuable to our use in invoking the gods and bringing forth Self — including the ancient percussive and vibrational instruments of the drum and the Aboriginal Australian *yidaki* (or didgeridoo), both of which are certainly the oldest instruments known. And recall that in the story of Dhruva, the great Rishi who instructs the child to use a mantra (in order to invoke the god) himself carries two musical instruments in his hands, a khartal and a tanpura, one instrument being stringed and one being percussive.

And this consideration leads us to another possible understanding suggested to us by the fact that the ancient traditions around the world preserve the stories and invocations of the gods in the form of chants, verses, and poetic meter, which is the fact that the gods themselves are also associated with the stars and planets and heavenly bodies (including of course the Sun and the Moon) which move along their courses in the sky in observable *cyclical* intervals. Rhythm is thus a very real connection between earth and heaven, and a way for us to bridge and open communication between the two.

The more I learn about the cycles of the heavens, and their harmonies and connections (unexplained under the conventional paradigm and typically either ignored or attributed to "coincidence"), such as the amazing harmonies between the cycles of the Moon, the Earth, and Venus, as well as other harmonies extending throughout the motions of all the great spheres of our system, the more I suspect that they are all influencing one another in ways that go beyond our current understanding of gravity, and that they are thus very likely influencing us in our lives in ways that have been studied by astrologers throughout the millennia but which are rejected and ridiculed by the modern materialist paradigm (and, we might observe, that have also been rejected and demonized by the literalist Christian hierarchies down through the centuries as well).

The harmonies and interactions of the heavenly spheres and their cycles, and in particular the potential central importance of our earth's Moon within the entire system as a kind of "central driveshaft," have been powerfully illustrated by the calculations and analysis of Simon Shack, who has proposed a variation of the solar system model of the great Danish astronomer Tycho Brahe (1546 – 1601).[104] Simon calls his modified version of Tycho Brahe's model the *Tychos model* (with the extra "s" added at the end to indicate *Simon Shack*).

If our Moon is in fact acting as a central driveshaft, with her orbits synchronized with the periods of all the other bodies in our system, from the Sun and Mercury all the way out to Pluto, as Simon has argued and observed (and as the makers of the so-called "Aztec Sun-Stone," which may come from the earlier people whom the Aztecs called the Toltec, seem to have also perceived and understood), this fact all by itself would expose grave flaws in the conventional model of our solar system, within which all these correspondences could only be dismissed as "coincidences," but of course that would be far too many supposed coincidences to simply ignore and dismiss — we would have to theorize that there are connections and harmonies going on which argue for influences that fall outside of our modern understanding and physics.

In contemplating this possibility, it is difficult not to hear the famous line of young Hamlet in Shakespeare's play, declaring: "There are more things in heaven and earth, Horatio, than are dreamt of in your philosophy" (*Hamlet* 1.5). And as we have already explored at some length, that play is based on recurring mythical patterns which echo down through the millennia, stretching back all the way to the earliest texts of ancient Egypt, and some earlier Germanic versions of the Hamlet legend furnished the title for that seminal 1969 book, *Hamlet's Mill*, which explored the connection of myth around the world and across the centuries, and whose authors suggest that the great mill-stone in question refers to the turning of the sky above the earth, grinding out the Ages as it does so.

In other words, I am now under the impression that the great rhythms of the heavens may well influence us in ways that are presently "undreamt of" in our dominant philosophies — or in our current understanding of physics and the nature of our solar system. And thus perhaps in order to know ourselves, and the influences of the various gods and goddesses upon our lives, our personalities, and our parts, it is also helpful to understand the positions of the planets and stars and the Sun and the Moon as they trace their paths inside this interrelated system which we ourselves occupy with them, the great heavenly givers of time and rhythm.

As we conclude, I am more convinced than ever that the ancient wisdom has been abandoned to our detriment, and that recovering the message imparted to our predecessors in the precious myths holds tremendous promise and potential blessing for our lives. Over the course of my ongoing journey into these ancient treasures, I have found teachings intended to benefit us on both the individual level and on the societal or national level as well.

The evidence is unmistakable that the ancient myths have as twin central themes both the opposition to oligarchy (and the exploitation by the few of the gifts and resources bestowed by the gods for the benefit of all) and the recovery of Self (recovery from trauma). In this volume we have not focused on the society-wide message of the myths, in their opposition to oligarchy — but instead have focused on their related central theme on the level of the individual, which is recovery of Self.

Through recovery of Self, and the harmonization of our various parts, and the healing and transformation of our exiles, we can best hope to live up to our own individual potential, and make fullest use of the gifts and talents and resources bestowed upon us individually — and in doing so, we will it is hoped benefit not only ourselves, but others around us, and the wider society of other men and women as well.

As we have seen in this volume, the more we can invoke Self and let Self shine forth, the more we will exhibit (because Self will exhibit) those attractive characteristics that Dr. Schwartz describes with the "Eight C's" of Compassion, Curiosity, Clarity, Creativity, Confidence, Courage, Connectedness, and Calm and the "Five P's" of Patience, Persistence, Presence, Perspective, and Playfulness. Trying to "imitate" these through the effort of parts who are trying to please society and garner external recognition not only proves to be futile and frustrating and even potentially despair-inducing, but also focuses our efforts on the praise and value "bestowed" by others, which is not only fickle and fluctuating even at the best of times, but also carries with it the message that our value is determined by those outside of us, which is false because we already have absolute intrinsic value and worth by virtue of the fact of being born into this life, possessed of an inborn and innate connection to the divine.

The practices and practical applications suggested in this book can all be seen as being geared towards relaxing and ultimately transforming those internal parts of our family who are desperately seeking external sources of valuing, because they have somehow taken up the toxic message that we are not already inherently valuable and possessed of an inner connection to the Infinite. That innate internal connection to the Infinite is embodied most powerfully in our deepest Self, and when we become alienated from Self then we are most vulnerable to need for external affirmations of value. The more we are experiencing and living in our authentic Self, the more we feel our own intrinsic value and our connection to the Infinite.

Thus, practices such as meditation are opportunities for us to visit with our various parts, and hear their concerns and their issues, and tell them calmly and lovingly that they can relax, that no one is threatening us right now, that no one is judging us right now, that indeed we value them and that in fact we already have intrinsic infinite value by virtue of simply being human, possessed of an unbreakable connection to the Infinite. As they relax and un-blend, Self can arise more and more clearly.

We have seen that there may be very ancient precedent for using the exercise of protruding the tongue as far as possible, while opening the eyes wide, in order to quickly activate our vagus nerve and calm inner voices of fear or panic, when we don't have time for a full meditation session or for chanting mantras or hymns. And we have seen that practices such as Wim Hof breath-work and Wim Hof cold-work, including cold showers and ice baths, can also be methods which give us opportunity to calm and comfort the voices of fearful parts and invoke Self to lead the entire internal family.

I am convinced that across the cultures of the world, our ancestors and predecessors have discovered and used and handed down countless other methods which all offer valid paths towards achieving the same goal, quieting the parts and invoking Self. Among these we could list the use of rhythmic drumming, rhythmic dancing, rhythmic instruments, rhythmic chanting and singing and recitation of mantras, performance of movements such as Yoga and Tai Chi and the ancient "Silk Reeling" exercises, and less formal practices including simply going out into nature.

Numerous ancient authors and surviving accounts testify to the tradition that an inscription at the famous Oracle at Delphi declared: "Know thyself." Various accounts add other inscriptions to accompany that one, but all the ancient traditions agree that the Oracle's primary inscription bore that command. Is it not significant that the one place most renowned for serving as the place where we receive the messages from the divine bore an inscription which directs us to know our Self?

As we make it a regular practice in our lives to invoke, and to trust in, our own true Self, we open ourselves to that power and inspiration, available to all men and women in this life.

And, as we recover our connection with Self, we will find that Self knows how to heal parts and enable them to put down their burdens and transform — just as the ancient myths demonstrate.

Thank you so much for taking this journey with me, and I wish you all success and blessing in your own exploration of the myths — and your own gods within.

Notes

1. *Point Break*. Dir. Kathryn Bigelow. *Largo Entertainment*, 1991.
2. *Ibid.*
3. *Ibid.*
4. Theogony of Hesiod. Trans. Hugh G. Evelyn-White, 1914.
    Sacred Texts. https://sacred-texts.com/cla/hesiod/theogony.htm
5. Bhagavata Purana, in the *Vishnu Parana*, trans. Horace Hayman Wilson, 1841.
    Sacred Texts. https://sacred-texts.com/hin/vp/vp009.htm
6. Mathisen, *Ancient World-Wide System.* See end note number 443 on pages 855 and 856.
7. From Buckley, *Odyssey Literally Translated*, page 109.
    https://archive.org/details/firstthirteenbooohomegoog/page/n115/mode/2up?view=theater
8. Duhalde, Marcelo, Yan Jing Tian and Dennis Wong, "Cantonese Performing Opera."
    In *South China Morning Post*, 08 November 2019.
    https://multimedia.scmp.com/infographics/culture/article/3036661/cantonese-opera/index.html
9. Liu, *Divine Threads*, 12 - 13.
10. *Ibid*, 13.
11. Teiwes, *Kachina Dolls*, 6.
12. Clews, *Pueblo Indian Religion*, 170.
13. Clark, Mary Ann. "Santería," in *Sects, Cults, and Spiritual Communities*, 124 - 125.
14. Bascom, *Sixteen Cowries*, 44.
15. *Ibid.*
16. *Journal of Joseph Banks*, 246 - 247.
17. Iyengar, *Light on Yoga*, 135 - 136.
18. *Ibid*, 135.
19. Lin, "Was Michael Jordan Controling his Vagus Nerve by Sticking Out his Tongue?"
20. Theogony, Trans. Evelyn-White, 233 - 236.
21. Ovid, *Heroides*, 203.
22. *Ibid.*
23. Apuleius, *Golden Ass*, Book Ten, section 33, translated directly from original.
24. Schwartz, *No Bad Parts*, 7.
25. *Ibid*, 13.
26. *Ibid*, 36.
27. *Ibid.*
28. *Orphic Hymns*, Trans. Athanassakis and Wolkow, 29 (page number, not Hymn number).
29. *Metamorphoses*, Ovid, Trans. Martin, 190.
30. *Ibid*, 189.
31. Kuhn, "Stable and the Manger," 4.
32. *No Bad Parts*, 15.
33. *Ibid*, 21.
34. Schwartz, "The Larger Self." https://ifs-institute.com/resources/articles/larger-self
35. *Ibid.*

36. *Orphic Hymns*, Trans. Athanassakis and Wolkow, 17.
37. *Ibid*, 21.
38. *Ibid*, 27.
39. *Ibid*, 13 - 14.
40. *Ibid*, 25 - 26.
41. *Ibid*, 53.
42. *Ibid*.
43. Iliad, Trans. Lattimore, 125.
44. Iliad, Trans. Buckley, 76.
45. Kingsley, *The Elders*.
46. Faulkner, *Requiem for a Nun*, 85.
47. Iliad, Trans. Buckley, 3 - 4.
48. Schwartz, "The Larger Self."
49. *No Bad Parts*, 22.
50. *Ibid*, 22 - 23.
51. *Ancient World-Wide System*, 346.
52. De Santillana and von Dechend, *Hamlet's Mill*, 146 - 147.
53. *Ibid*, 222.
54. Theogony, Trans. Most, 17 - 18.
55. *Hamlet's Mill*, 58 and 62 (58 to first ellipses in quotation).
56. Plutarch. *De Faciae quae in Orbe Lunae Apparet*.
57. *Hamlet's Mill*, 46, 418.
58. *Ibid*, 418.
59. Hancock, *Fingerprints of the Gods*, 54.
60. *Ibid*.
61. *Ibid*, 51.
62. *No Bad Parts*, 29.
63. *Ibid*, 30 - 31.
64. Odyssey, Trans. Fagles, 408.
65. Eliade, *Shamanism*, 435.
66. Hof, *Wim Hof Method*, 38.
67. "Dr. Laurence Heller in Conversation with Dr. Gabor Maté," *Transforming Trauma Podcast*.
68. *Ibid*.
69. "Dr. Gabor Maté on Childhood Trauma, The Real Cause of Anxiety, and our 'Insane' Culture." *Human Window Podcast*.
70. Bowlby, *Separation*, 200.
71. *No Bad Parts*, 74.
72. *Separation*, 27 and 74.
73. *Ibid*, 22.
74. Levine, *Healing Trauma*, 7.
75. *An Officer and a Gentleman*. Dir. Taylor Hackford, Lorimar: 1982.
76. Theogony, Trans. Wenger, 32.
77. Ovid, *Metamorphoses*, end of Book 4 (or Liber IV).
78. *Metamorphoses*, Latin text from Latin Library. https://www.thelatinlibrary.com/ovid/ovid.met4.shtml
79. Described in Theogony, lines 270ff.
80. *No Bad Parts*, 75, quoting Bly, *Little Book on the Human Shadow*, 19.

81. Bly, *Little Book on the Human Shadow*, 19.
82. *Ibid*, 74.
83. Schwartz, *Internal Family Systems*, 6.
84. *No Bad Parts*, 89.
85. *Ibid*, 17.
86. *Ibid*, 63.
87. *Ibid*, 19.
88. *Ibid*, 161.
89. *Ibid*, 90, 92.
90. Spurgeon, "The agreement of salvation by faith with walking in good works."
91. *Ibid*.
92. Massey, "Paul the Gnostic Opponent of Peter, not a supporter of Historical Christianity."
93. *Ibid*.
94. *Ibid*.
95. *Ibid*.
96. *Ibid*.
97. Taylor, *Devil's Pulpit*, 145 - 160.
98. Nalaka Sutta, Trans. Thānissaro Bhikkhu.
99. *Ibid*.
100. Tao Te Ching, Trans. Mair, 138.
101. *Ibid*, 141 - 142.
102. Orphic Hymns, Trans. Athanassakis and Wolkow, xx - xxi.
103. *Ibid*, xix.
104. Shack, *Tychos, Second Edition*, Chapter 13. https://book.tychos.space/chapters/13-the-central-driveshaft

Image Credits

L isted by page number. Star-charts created by the author using the free open-source planetarium app, Stellarium (stellarium.org).

16. Vishnu dreaming the universe, Wikimedia commons.
    https://commons.wikimedia.org/wiki/File:Vishnu_and_Lakshmi_on_Shesha_Naga,_ca_1870.jpg

17. Vishnu and Dhruva, Wikimedia commons.
    https://commons.wikimedia.org/wiki/File:Story_of_dhruva.jpg

29. Left: Zeus and Typhon, Wikimedia commons.
    https://commons.wikimedia.org/wiki/File:Combat_de_Zeus_contre_Typhon.jpg
    Right: Maya drinking vessel with artwork depicting Chahk.
    https://www.metmuseum.org/art/collection/search/310364

33. Two screenshots from YouTube videos showing dancers.
    Top: https://www.youtube.com/watch?v=do-bNDaxgR8
    Bottom: https://www.youtube.com/watch?v=-SOmaCLaYs4

35. Statue of Zao Gongen, Wikimedia commons.
    https://commons.wikimedia.org/wiki/File:蔵王権現立像-Zaō_Gongen_MET_DT5160.jpg

36. Gorgon artwork on an ancient vase, Wikimedia commons.
    https://commons.wikimedia.org/wiki/File:Gorgon_Louvre_F230.jpg Gorgon on a vase at the Louvre

37. Gorgon artwork on an ancient plate, Wikimedia commons.
    https://commons.wikimedia.org/wiki/File:Gorgon_Kameiros_BM_GR1860.4-4.2.jpg Rhodes Gorgon

38. Maori haka in North Africa, Wikimedia commons.
    https://commons.wikimedia.org/wiki/File:E_003261_E_Maoris_in_North_Africa_July_1941.jpg Maori Haka

40. Carving of Tiki, Wikimedia commons.
    https://commons.wikimedia.org/wiki/File:Tiki_Pukana_(7713925362).jpg

44. Two images of Simhasana, Wikimedia commons.
    Left: https://commons.wikimedia.org/wiki/File:Simhasana_Yoga-Asana_Nina-Mel.jpg
    Right: https://commons.wikimedia.org/wiki/File:Mr-yoga-lion-pose-in-garland-pose.jpg

45. Relief of Narasimha, Wikimedia commons.
https://commons.wikimedia.org/wiki/File:Narasimha_killing_Hiranya.JPG

46. Statue of Bes, Wikimedia commons.
https://commons.wikimedia.org/wiki/File:Egypt.Dendera.Bes.01.jpg

94. Joseph Reveals his Dream, Wikimedia commons.
https://commons.wikimedia.org/wiki/File:Tissot_Joseph_Reveals_His_Dream_to_His_Brethren.jpg

102. Woman winnowing grain, Wikimedia commons.
https://commons.wikimedia.org/wiki/File:Rice_winnowing,_Uttarakhand,_India.jpg

112. Saturn Statue in Frankfurt, Wikimedia commons.
https://commons.wikimedia.org/wiki/File:Senckenbergmuseum_Frankfurt_2.jpg

136. From video taken by Madelyn Jansen, 2023.

151. Two ancient pieces depicting Athena, Wikimedia commons.
Top (ancient pottery): https://commons.wikimedia.org/wiki/File:Athena_owl_Met_09.221.43.jpg
Bottom (ancient sculpture): https://commons.wikimedia.org/wiki/File:001MA_Athena.jpg

154. Athena and Heracles, Wikimedia commons.
https://commons.wikimedia.org/wiki/File:Oedipus_Painter_ARV_441_185_Herakles_and_Athena_-_Peleus_subduing_Thetis_(01).jpg

164. Athena and Perseus, Wikimedia commons.
https://commons.wikimedia.org/wiki/File:Terracotta_pelike_(jar)_MET_DT352033.jpg

166. Two ancient pieces depicting Perseus and Harpe Sword, Wikimedia commons.
Left: https://commons.wikimedia.org/wiki/File:Perseus_Achilles_Painter_Louvre_CA6106.jpg
Right: https://commons.wikimedia.org/wiki/File:Berlin_Painter_ARV_197_11_Gorgo_pursuing_Perseus_(06).jpg

186. Two depictions of the Roman god Janus, Wikimedia commons.
Left: https://commons.wikimedia.org/wiki/File:Janus,_the_Roman_god_(1550).jpg
Right: https://commons.wikimedia.org/wiki/File:Janus,_the_Roman_god_(1878).jpg

189. Painting of Peter with Keys (top),
Image of Key Nomenclature (bottom), Wikimedia commons.
Peter with keys: Peter with Keys: https://commons.wikimedia.org/wiki/File:Pope-peter_pprubens.jpg
Key nomenclature: https://commons.wikimedia.org/wiki/File:Lever_lock_key_parts.svg

199. Buddha under tree with Vajrapani, Wikimedia commons.
https://commons.wikimedia.org/wiki/File:Buddha-Vajrapani-Herakles.JPG

Bibliography

Apuleius. *The Golden Ass: Being the Metamorphoses of Lucius Apuleius.*
Latin Text with accompanying English Translation by W. Adlington.
London: Heinemann, 1922.

Banks, Joseph. *Journal of the Right Honourable Sir Joseph Banks, During Captain Cook's First Voyage in HMS* Endeavour *in 1768-71*. Joseph D. Hooker, ed.
London: MacMillan, 1896.

Bascom, William R. *Sixteen Cowries: Yoruba Divination from Africa to the New World.*
Bloomington: University of Indiana Press, 1980.

Bly, Robert. *A Little Book on the Human Shadow.* San Francisco: Harper and Row, 1988.

Bowlby, John. *Separation: Anxiety and Anger.* In *Attachment and Loss* (volume 2).
New York: Basic Books, 1973.

De Santillana, Giorgio and Hertha von Dechend. *Hamlet's Mill:
An essay on myth and the frame of time.* Boston: Nonpareil, 1969.

Duhalde, Marcelo, Yan Jing Tian and Dennis Wong, "Cantonese Performing Opera."
In *South China Morning Post*, 08 November 2019.
https://multimedia.scmp.com/infographics/culture/article/3036661/cantonese-opera/index.html

Eliade, Mircea. *Shamanism: Archaic Techniques of Ecstasy.* Trans. William R. Trask. 1964.
Princeton: Bollingen, 1972.

Faulkner, William. *Requiem for a Nun.* London: Chatto & Windus, 1919.

Hancock, Graham. *Fingerprints of the Gods.* New York: Three Rivers Press, 1995.

Heller, Laurence and Gabor Maté. "Dr. Laurence Heller in Conversation with Dr. Gabor Maté
on Complex Trauma and the Future of Trauma-Informed Care." Interview with Sarah Buino.
Transforming Trauma Podcast. https://narmtraining.com/transformingtrauma/episode-007/

Hesiod. *The Homeric Hymns and Homerica.* Trans. Hugh G. Evelyn-White,
London: Heinemann, 1914.

Hesiod. *Theogony, Works and Days.* Trans. Dorothea Wenger. New York: Penguin, 1972.

Hesiod. *Theogony, Works and Days, Testimonia.* Trans. Glenn W. Most.
Cambridge: Harvard University Press, 2006.

Hof, Wim. *The Wim Hof Method: Activate Your Potential, Transcend Your Limits.*
London: Rider, 2020.

Homer. Iliad. Trans. Theodore Alois Buckley. *Iliad of Homer, Literally Translated with Explanatory Notes*. London: Henry G. Bohn, 1861.
https://archive.org/details/iliadofhomerlite00homeuoft/page/n7/mode/2up

Homer, Iliad. Trans. Richard Lattimore. *Iliad of Homer*. Chicago: University of Chicago Press, 1961.

Homer. Odyssey. Trans. Theodore Alois Buckley. *First Thirteen Books of the Odyssey of Homer, Literally Translated with Explanatory Notes*. Philadelphia: David McKay, 1896.
https://archive.org/details/firstthirteenboo0homegoog/page/n115/mode/2up?view=theater

Homer. Odyssey. Trans. Robert Fagles. *The Odyssey*. New York: Viking Penguin, 1996.

Iyengar, B.K.S. *Light on Yoga: Yoga Dipika*. rev. ed. NY: Schocken, 1966.

Kingsley, Peter. *The Elders* (recorded lectures).
https://peterkingsley.org/product/the-elders/

Kuhn, Alvin Boyd. "The Stable and the Manger." 1936.
https://archive.org/details/TheStableAndTheManger

Lao Tzu. *Tao Te Ching: The Classic Book of Integrity and the Way*. Trans. Victor H. Mair. NY: Bantam, 1990.

Levine, Peter. *Healing Trauma: A Pioneering Program for Restoring the Wisdom of Your Body*. Boulder: Sounds True, 2008.

Lin, Steven. "Was Michael Jordan Controling his Vagus Nerve by Sticking Out his Tongue?" Facebook post, 19 September 2021.
https://www.facebook.com/DrStevenLin/posts/was-micheal-jordan-controlling-his-vagus-nerve-by-sticking-out-his-tonguefor-a-p/389928439360835/

Liu, April. *Divine Threads: The Visual and Material Culture of Cantonese Opera*. Vancouver: University of British Columbia, 2019.

Tao Te Ching: The Classic Book of Integrity and the Way. Lao Tzu, trans. Victor H. Mair. NY: Bantam, 1990. 138

Massey, Gerald. "Paul the Gnostic Opponent of Peter, not a supporter of Historical Christianity." In *Ten Bound Lectures*. 1900. https://archive.org/details/GeraldMassey-Lectures/page/n21/mode/2up

Maté, Gabor. "Dr. Gabor Maté on Childhood Trauma, The Real Cause of Anxiety, and our 'Insane' Culture." Interview with Martin Caparrotta. *Human Window*, July 2019; Transcript published 23 November 2019.

Mathisen, David Warner. *Ancient World-Wide System: Star Myths of the World, Volume One. Second edition*. Paso Robles: Beowulf, 2019.

Mathisen, David Warner. *Myth and Trauma: Higher Self, Ancient Wisdom, and their Enemies*. Paso Robles: Beowulf, 2020.

Mathisen, David Warner. *Star Myths of the World, Volume Two: Myths of Ancient Greece*. Paso Robles: Beowulf, 2016.

"Nalaka Sutta: To Nalaka. (Sn 3.11)" Trans. Thānissaro Bhikkhu. *Access to Insight*. 2013.
https://www.accesstoinsight.org/tipitaka/kn/snp/snp.3.11.than.html

Officer and a Gentleman. Dir. Taylor Hackford, Lorimar: 1982.

Orphic Hymns. Trans. Apostolos N. Athanassakis and Benjamin M. Wolkow. Baltimore: Johns Hopkins University Press, 2013.

Ovid. *Heroides and Amores*. Trans. Grant Showerman. London: Heinemann, 1914.

Ovid. *Metamorphoses* (Latin text). *The Latin Library*. https://www.thelatinlibrary.com/ovid/ovid.met4.shtml

Ovid. *Metamorphoses*. Trans. Charles Martin. New York: Norton, 2004.

Parsons, Elsie Clews. *Pueblo Indian Religion, Volume 1*. Lincoln: University of Nebraska Press, 1939.

Petrowsky, Marc and William W. Zellner, eds. *Sects, Cults, and Spiritual Communites: A Sociological Analysis*. Westport, CT: Praeger, 1998.

Plutarch. *De Faciae quae in Orbe Lunae Apparet.* Trans. William Watson Goodwin. Boston: Little, Brown, 1874. https://catalog.perseus.org/catalog/urn:cts:greekLit:tlg0007.tlg126.perseus-eng1

Point Break. Dir. Kathryn Bigelow. Largo Entertainment, 1991.

Schwartz, Richard C. "The Larger Self." nd. https://ifs-institute.com/resources/articles/larger-self

Schwartz, Richard C. *No Bad Parts: Healing Trauma & Restoring Wholeness with the Internal Family Systems Model.* Boulder: Sounds True, 2021.

Schwartz, Richard C. *Internal Family Systems.* Boulder: Sounds True, 2023.

Shack, Simon. *The Tychos: Our Geoaxial Binary System, Second Edition.* March, 2022. https://book.tychos.space

Spurgeon, Charles H. "The agreement of salvation by faith with walking in good works." Sermon. 28 June, 1891. https://archive.spurgeon.org/sermons/2210.php

Taylor, Robert. *The Astronomico-Theological Lectures of the Rev. Robert Taylor, B.A.* New York: Calvin Blanchard, 1857.

Taylor, Robert. *The Devil's Pulpit: or Astro-Theological Sermons by the Rev. Robert Taylor, B.A.* New York: Calvin Blanchard, 1857.

Teiwes, Helga. *Kachina Dolls: The Art of Hopi Carvers.* Tucson: University of Arizona Press, 1991.

Index